Architecture in the Age of Artificial Intelligence

T0281827

Architecture in the Age of Artificial Intelligence

An introduction to AI for architects

NEIL LEACH

BLOOMSBURY VISUAL ARTS
LONDON · NEW YORK · OXFORD · NEW DELHI · SYDNEY

BLOOMSBURY VISUAL ARTS
Bloomsbury Publishing Plc
50 Bedford Square, London, WC1B 3DP, UK
1385 Broadway, New York, NY 10018, USA
29 Earlsfort Terrace, Dublin 2, Ireland

BLOOMSBURY, BLOOMSBURY VISUAL ARTS and the Diana logo are
trademarks of Bloomsbury Publishing Plc

First published in Great Britain 2022
Reprinted 2023

Cover design by Namkwan Cho and Eleanor Rose
Cover image © Refik Anadol

A catalogue record for this book is available from the British Library.

Library of Congress Cataloging-in-Publication Data
Names: Leach, Neil, author.
Title: Architecture in the age of artificial intelligence : an introduction
for architects / Neil Leach.
Identifiers: LCCN 2021011458 (print) | LCCN 2021011459 (ebook) |
ISBN 9781350165519 (paperback) | ISBN 9781350165526 (hardback) |
ISBN 9781350165533 (pdf) | ISBN 9781350165540 (epub) |
ISBN 9781350165557
Subjects: LCSH: Architecture and technology. | Artificial intelligence.
Classification: LCC NA2543.T43 L43 2021 (print) | LCC NA2543.T43 (ebook)
| DDC 720.1/05—dc23
LC record available at https://lccn.loc.gov/2021011458
LC ebook record available at https://lccn.loc.gov/2021011459

ISBN: HB: 978-1-3501-6552-6
        PB: 978-1-3501-6551-9
        ePDF: 978-1-3501-6553-3
        eBook: 978-1-3501-6554-0

Typeset by RefineCatch Limited, Bungay, Suffolk
Printed and bound in Great Britain

To find out more about our authors and books visit www.bloomsbury.com
and sign up for our newsletters.

Contents

Illustrations

Plates

Figures

Acknowledgements

Books seldom come out of nowhere. Often they are the product of several years of reflecting on a particular issue. I cannot be sure where this particular book germinated, although I am tempted to think that the initial seeds were planted in the countless hours spent in the Computer Science Laboratory, perched above the Babbage Lecture Theatre at the University of Cambridge back in the late 1980s. This is where I worked on the translation of Alberti's treatise on architecture, *de re aedificatoria*, using the mainframe university computer, surrounded by highly talented students of Computer Science.[1]

This book has been many years in the making. It has been a long journey. I am grateful to all who have accompanied me on this journey, to colleagues and students from the Architectural Association, Harvard Graduate School of Design (GSD), Southern California Institute of Architecture (SCI-Arc), Institute of Advanced Architecture of Catalunya (IAAC), Dessau Institute of Architecture (DIA), Tongji University, Florida International University (FIU) and many other institutions along the way. I am especially grateful to the DigitalFUTURES community that has done so much to host workshops and debates about AI. I am also very grateful both to the remarkably talented group of students on the Doctor of Design (DDes) program at FIU and to those who have joined our discussions on that program.

In particular, I would like to thank Daniel Bolojan, Wolf Prix, Wanyu He, Theodoros Galanos, Immanuel Koh, Marina Rodriguez das Neves, Soomeen Hahm, Philippe Morel, Patrik Schumacher, Behnaz Farahi, Biayna Bogosian, Matias del Campo, Refik Anadol, Anil Seth, Andy Clark, Shajay Bhooshan, Mark Burry, Kostas Terzidis, Virginia Melnyk, Gustavo Rincon, Ahmed Hassab, Nic Bao, Mohammed Behjoo, Claudiu Barsan Pipu, Shima Beigi, Manos Vermisso, Shermeen Yousif, Jorge Tubella, Alessio Erioli, Sanford Kwinter, Manuel DeLanda, Ciro Najle, Claudia Pasquero, Niccolo Casas, Maria Kuptsova, Sina

Mostafavi, Sang Lee, Aleksandra Jaeschke, Viktoria Luisa Barbo, Antoine Picon, Marrikka Trotter, Thom Mayne, Ben Bratton, Philip Yuan, Chao Yan, Shen Jie, Roland Snooks, Gilles Retsin, Achim Menges, Philippe Block, Mike Xie, Areti Markoloulou, Mette Thomsen, Memo Akten, Lev Manovich, Guvenc Ozel, Benjamin Ennemoser, Darren Ockert, Sofia Crespo, Aya Riad, Jason Chandler, John Stuart, John Stein, Anna Nikolaidou, Rosemary Wilson and Adam Dixon. I would also like to thank those who contributed material to this book, and to members of the highly professional team at Bloomsbury, especially my editors, James Thompson and Alexander Highfield, who have seen it through to completion.

Preface

Attitudes to artificial intelligence (AI) remain remarkably polarised. For some it is a tool with extraordinary potential to make life easier in the future. As Alan Turing wrote of computation in general, 'This is only a foretaste of what is to come, and only a shadow of what is going to be.'[1] Meanwhile for others, AI itself poses an existential threat to human civilization. As Stephen Hawking warns us, 'The development of full artificial intelligence could spell the end of the human race.'[2]

In this sense, AI is a two-edged sword. It has potential for both good and evil. AI poses a dilemma, and no one sums up this dilemma better than Elon Musk. On the one hand, Musk is himself developing AI-based tools for his commercial ventures, from the now well established Tesla car company to the still speculative Neuralink project. On the other hand, Musk is only too aware of the potential dangers it poses: 'I think we should be very careful about artificial intelligence. If I were to guess like what our biggest existential threat is, it's probably that. So we need to be very careful with the artificial intelligence . . . With artificial intelligence we are summoning the demon.'[3] Stuart Russell faces a similar dilemma. Although he is one of the pioneers of AI, and co-author of the influential book, *Artificial Intelligence: A Modern Approach*, he has also commissioned an arms control video warning us of the dangers of 'slaughterbots', autonomous AI controlled drones that can kill.[4]

This series reflects this paradox. This first volume, *Architecture in the Age of Artificial Intelligence*, is a celebration of the positive contributions of AI. It outlines the extraordinary achievements of AI in the past, and speculates about the potential of AI to design buildings for us in the future. By contrast, the second volume, *The Death of the Architect*, exposes the potential dark side of AI, and outlines the risks that it poses in terms of unemployment, surveillance and the loss of personal freedom.

These first two volumes are intended as a dialectical foil to each other. There is no presumption that one should be more persuasive than the other. It is left to readers to form their own opinions, based on the arguments in both volumes. In some senses, however, the arguments are actually the same. They are just two sides of the same coin. Once AI is able to design buildings for us, will this not lead to 'The Death of the Architect'?

Neil Leach, Venice Beach, California

Introduction

AI is now very much part of our lives, even though we might not realise it.

AI identifies our friends on FaceBook, and categorises our images on Instagram. It feeds us news and advertisements based on our online histories. It filters our email spam. It suggests how we should end of our sentences. It translates foreign texts. It opens our phones. It feeds us music on Spotify, and movies on Netflix. It even introduces us to our potential partners.

AI has colonised our homes in the form of Siri, Alexa, Cortana and Google Assistant.[1] It monitors our heating, and checks the quality of our water.[2] It controls robots that clean our floors.[3] It pays our bills, helps us with our taxes, reminds us of our appointments, and schedules our meetings. In some cases it allows us to pay for our goods through facial recognition, and to even board our planes. It is embedded throughout the fabric of our cities, monitoring them and making them more efficient and sustainable.

AI also warns us, when driving, if we stray out of lane. It controls self-driving cars, buses and trucks. It pays our tolls with transponders and vehicle identification systems. It shows us the fastest route and tells us where to park.[4] It is transforming how we shop, order rides and organise our lives.

All of a sudden, AI is everywhere.

But it is not as though we even notice it. AI does not look like a robot. In fact it does not look like anything at all. With AI, think algorithms, not robots. AI is completely invisible. AI controls the environment around us. Even though we might not even realise it, AI has already infiltrated our lives. And its influence is growing every day.

It is as though the Earth has been invaded by an invisible, super intelligent, alien species.[5]

AI and architecture

What impact will AI have on architecture?

There are several areas where AI is already having a major impact on architectural culture. Its most noticeable impact has been in academic circles, where AI has burst onto the scene in design studios in certain progressive schools of architecture.[6] Although the most popular AI techniques were discovered only recently, interest in them has begun to spread like wildfire. Inspirational images of buildings and urban design proposals are now being generated automatically by a process often referred to as 'hallucination', a term that also evokes the seemingly hallucinatory nature of the images generated. AI generated work is starting to attract considerable interest,[7] while workshops and tutorials for generating AI based designs have also become immensely popular.[8]

'It is as though the Earth has been invaded by an invisible, super intelligent, alien species.'

AI has also become a hot topic in academic research conferences.[9] It has become a popular field for doctoral research, especially in technologically advanced institutions, such as MIT Media Lab.[10] Several academic courses and even programmes now focus specifically on AI.[11] Within a few years we can expect AI-based courses in every single discipline.

AI is also having a major impact in the world of galleries and exhibitions. The first exhibition of AI generated artworks was held in

FIGURE 0.1 Casey Rehm (Ishida Rehm Studio), *Automatic Ginza*, '3 Ways' exhibition, A+D Museum, Los Angeles, California (2018). This image is a still taken from a video that uses a neural network trained on a video of the Ginza district in Tokyo taken by a mobile phone to transform 2D greyscale rectangles into an architectural façade.

2017, and the first auction of an AI generated artwork in 2018. And architecture is not far behind. The first exhibition of AI generated architectural designs was held in 2019. There has been considerable interest in AI generated work online, with regular postings on Instagram, Facebook, WeChat and other social media platforms.

AI is also starting to have an impact on progressive architectural practice. An increasing number of high-profile architects are starting to incorporate new AI based techniques into their design strategies. Pritzker Prize winner Thom Mayne, of Morphosis, has begun to explore the potential of AI to increase the range of design options. Wolf Prix of Coop Himmelb(l)au has used it to improve the design process. Meanwhile Patrik Schumacher of Zaha Hadid Architects (ZHA) has used it to simulate the behaviour of occupants in his buildings.

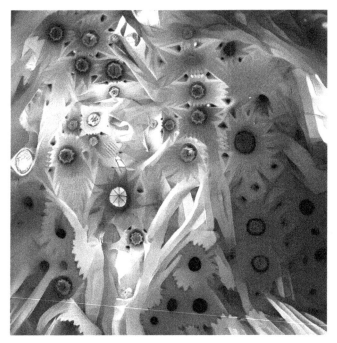

FIGURE 0.2 Daniel Bolojan, *Machine Perceptions: Gaudí + Neural Networks* (2020). This project uses CycleGANs not to transfer one domain's style to another, but rather to transfer one domain's underlying compositional characteristics to another domain. The neural network learns to discriminate towards less relevant compositional features while enhancing the relevant ones, in a similar way to how humans learn, by sorting and filtering irrelevant information.

AI is already embedded in standard architectural software, although most architects are probably not aware of it. Established commercial companies, such as Autodesk, are now beginning to integrate more advanced AI into their software, while a number of startups, such as Xkool and Spacemaker AI, are developing new AI-based software tools for architects and developers.[12] AI is proving capable of processing complex site information, and offering a greater range of design options, maximising the potential of any given site. In addition, AI is now being used to control robotic fabrication technologies and to improve the performance of buildings once constructed.

And yet we are still in the early stages of the AI revolution. Ben Bratton has described how we are still in the 'silent movies' period of computation, and AI is but a recent development within the longer history of computation. But there is a lot more to come. AI is certain to become an integral part of our future, and will undoubtedly prove to be a powerful aid in augmenting human design abilities and speeding up the design process. The writing is on the wall.

By the end of this decade, we could predict that there will not be a single profession or discipline left untouched by AI. And architecture will be no exception. Thanks to AI, the very practice of architectural design will be completely overhauled, and so will architectural education.

Beyond technophobia

Not everyone will be so positive about the introduction of AI into architecture. Some will dismiss it, just as some dismissed computers when first introduced into mainstream architectural culture some thirty years ago. Why use computers, they would ask, when human beings can draw so much better? Why use artificial intelligence, some will no doubt ask, when we have human intelligence? Equally, others might even be even more critical, dismissing AI as part of a 'New Dark Age', or a vital cog in 'surveillance capitalism'.[13]

This is perhaps understandable. After all, how often do we see robots and computers portrayed in a negative light in popular culture? From *Metropolis* onwards, many movies cast robots as evil artificial life forms that pose a threat to humankind. Take *2001: A Space Odyssey*, where Hal, the sentient supercomputer controlling a space flight to Jupiter, eventually turns against the astronauts on board. Or take the *Terminator* movies, where Skynet, the often invisible, super-intelligent AI system, plays the main antagonist. Or take *Blade Runner*, where bio-engineered robots infiltrate their way seamlessly into human society, causing mayhem.

This distrust of robots and computers in the movies can be understood within the broader context of technophobia in general that can also be traced back to some of the more conservative approaches in philosophy that still inform architectural theory. One problem with philosophy, as Stephen Hawking famously observes, is that too often it fails to keep pace with technology.[14] But another problem with philosophy is that it is often antagonistic towards technology.

Martin Heidegger, for example, sees technology as a potential source of alienation.[15] He fails to appreciate, however, the gradual way in which we appropriate new technologies through a form of proprioception.[16] Think of the outrage caused by Le Corbusier's famous description of the house as 'a machine for living in'. But do we not now live in houses bristling with technological devices of every kind? The same goes for engineering. Take the Eiffel Tower. When first constructed, many Parisians regarded it as an unspeakably ugly edifice. Indeed, Guy de Maupassant would frequently take his lunch at a restaurant in the Eiffel Tower, even though he was not so fond of the food there, on the basis that it was the only place in Paris from which he could not see the tower.[17] And yet the Eiffel Tower has now become a much-loved symbol of Paris. Heidegger's anti-technological stance now seems radically out of place in a world where technology has colonised our horizon of consciousness, where we not only accept technology, but even start connecting with it from an emotional perspective. How long is it before we become attached to our laptops, and give our cars names?[18] Isn't time to *forget* Heidegger?[19]

The prosthetic imagination

For a more nuanced philosophical understanding of how we adapt to technology, and absorb it so that it becomes a prosthetic extension to our own bodies, we should perhaps turn to Maurice Merleau-Ponty, who recognises that any tool can eventually be appropriated as part of our extended body schema, so that we come to experience the world *through* our tools.[20] Think of a blind person who has to navigate the world using a white cane. Eventually the cane becomes 'invisible' as it is absorbed into the extended sense of the embodied self.[21] The same happens with cars. With time we become so familiar with the operations of driving – accelerating, braking, steering and so on – that they fade into the background to become part of our subconscious such that we come to drive *through* our cars. And something similar happens with the spaces we inhabit. The initial sense of displacement or alienation that we might feel when first moving into a new apartment or house gradually fades away, and over time we become attached to it and start to feel at home there.[22]

Andy Clark and David Chalmers take this idea even further and argue that a tool can even become part of our 'extended mind'.[23] Take the mobile phone. Instead of memorising phone numbers, we now keep those numbers on our mobile phone. Our social contacts are stored there. Our whole lives are contained there. Our 'cellphones' have become our 'self-phones'. We have absorbed our mobile phones and other external devices at a symbolic level, so that they have become part of who we are. They have become prosthetic extensions of our minds.

Katherine Hayles then goes one step further still. Why limit ourselves to the human mind, when the whole body has been augmented by the increasing introduction of these new technologies? For Hayles, we cannot separate the mind from the body, as though the mind is simply housed in the body.[24] The mind is precisely part of the body. Moreover, as Hayles points out, the body has indeed been extended by these new technologies, such that the traditional concept of 'humanism' – the notion that the human body can be perceived as a discrete unit in and of itself – has now become untenable. For Hayles, then, we need to go so far as to challenge the traditional liberal concept of humanism and accept that we now operate within a 'posthuman condition'.[25]

Cyborg culture

The term 'cyborg' was first coined to refer to the potential of enhancing the human body in order for it to survive in extraterrestrial environments.[26] More recently, however, it has been deployed by Donna Haraway to refer to a cybernetic organism, 'a hybrid of machine and organism, a creature of social reality as well as a creature of fiction'.[27] Moreover, this hybrid condition should be understood not as static, but as one that is continually adapting and mutating: 'Already in the few decades that they have existed, they have mutated, in fact and fiction, into second-order entities like genomic and electronic databases and the other denizens of the zone called cyberspaces.'[28] As such, we have now evolved, so that the cyborg has become our predominant disposition: 'By the late twentieth century, our time, a mythic time, we are all chimeras, theorized and fabricated hybrids of machine and organism; in short, we are cyborgs.'[29]

Although this notion of the cyborg might conjure up images of technologically enhanced human bodies, such as Terminator or Eve 8, a cyborg does not actually depend on advanced technology. Forget the romanticised notion of the cyborg – half human, half robot – that we see in the movies. A cyborg is simply a creature that uses any form of prosthesis. An ordinary walking stick is a prosthesis.[30] As Clark comments:

> The cyborg is a potent cultural icon of the late twentieth century. It conjures images of human–machine hybrids and the physical merging of flesh and electronic circuitry. My goal is to hijack that image and to reshape it, revealing it as a disguised vision of (oddly) our own biological nature. For what is special about human brains, and what best explains the distinctive features of human intelligence, is precisely their ability to enter into deep and complex relationships with nonbiological constructs, props, and aids.

The usefulness of these 'constructs, props and aids', however, is determined by their affordances – their potential uses – which remain constrained by our own capabilities. A tool, after all, is no use, if we cannot use it. Likewise a tool might 'lend itself' to certain operations, but not to others.[31] A tool, however, has no agency.[32] It cannot force us to use it in a certain way. Nonetheless, with an appropriate tool, the capacity of human beings can be enhanced considerably.

As such, as Elon Musk has commented, 'All of us already are cyborgs.'[33] It is, moreover, our increasing reliance on sophisticated digital prostheses that is making us ever more cyborg-like.[34] These digital prostheses are enhancing our abilities, such that they have begun to make us 'superhuman'. Musk again: 'You have a machine extension of yourself in the form of your phone, and your computer and all your applications. You are already superhuman.'[35]

It is precisely our capacity to adapt so effectively to new tools that, for Clark, makes human beings 'natural born cyborgs'.[36] We are naturally adaptive creatures, because our brains are themselves so adaptive. Neuroscientists tell us that the human brain is 'plastic'.[37] The brain has the capacity to adapt constantly to ever changing circumstances, and it is its very 'plasticity' that gives human beings the capacity to appropriate new technologies so that they become part of our extended sense of self: 'It is the presence of this unusual plasticity that makes humans (but not dogs, cats, or elephants) natural-born cyborgs: beings primed by Mother Nature to annex wave upon wave of external elements and structures as part and parcel of their own extended minds.'[38]

Moreover, for Clark, this is why cyborg culture does not make us post-human, but rather affirms us as being quintessentially human, in that the innate capacity to adapt plays such a significant role in what it is to be human. This, then, allows Clark to challenge Hayles's claim that we have become post-human: 'Such extensions should not be thought of as rendering us in any way post-human; not because they are not deeply transformative but because we humans are naturally designed to be the subjects of just such repeated transformations!'[39]

Extended intelligence

It is in the context of this burgeoning 'cyborg culture' – where humans have been augmented to become superhuman – that we can explore the full potential of AI as being not an end in itself, but a prosthetic device that can enhance the natural intelligence of the human being. For if the mind – or indeed the embodied self – can be extended through the phone and other devices, could we not also argue that intelligence itself can be enhanced through artificial intelligence?

Increasingly nowadays we are hearing references not to straightforward 'artificial intelligence' but to 'extended intelligence' (EI). Ultimately, the most productive strategy is to see the relationship between AI and human intelligence not as one of competition, but rather as a potential synergy between the two, whereby AI operates in tandem with human intelligence and becomes an *extension* to human intelligence. As Joi Ito puts it:

> Instead of thinking about machine intelligence in terms of humans vs. machines, we should consider the system that integrates humans and machines – not artificial intelligence, but extended intelligence. Instead of trying to control or design or even

understand systems, it is more important to design systems that participate as responsible, aware and robust elements of even more complex systems. And we must question and adapt our own purpose and sensibilities as designers and components of the system for a much more humble approach: Humility over Control. We could call it 'participant design' – design of systems as and by participants – that is more akin to the increase of a flourishing function, where flourishing is a measure of vigor and health rather than scale or power. We can measure the ability for systems to adapt creatively, as well as their resilience and their ability to use resources in an interesting way.[40]

An alternative way of understanding this coupling of human and AI is as a form of 'intelligence augmentation (IA)'. As Anant Jhingran comments, 'AI makes machines autonomous and detached from humans; IA, in on the other hand, puts humans in control and leverages computing power to amplify our capabilities.'[41] Whether we call it 'extended intelligence' or 'intelligence augmentation', the basic concept of coupling human intelligence with AI remains the same. As such, we should not be referring to AI in isolation, so much as a potential extension or augmentation of human intelligence.[42] This extended or augmented intelligence – this synergy between our bodies and machines – will undoubtedly prove enormously productive.[43] As Yann Lecunn observes, 'Our intelligence is what makes us smarter, and AI is an extension of that quality.'[44]

An introduction to AI

This is an introductory book outlining what AI can contribute to the discipline of architecture. As such, it does not go into any great detail. Rather it offers an overview of what is a fascinating and increasingly relevant topic. It tries to describe in a few broad brushstrokes how AI operates, how it has developed and what potential it holds for the future of architecture. It should be noted, however, that this book is no technical manual. It does not offer any technical instructions as to how to use AI.[45] Nor does it attempt to provide a comprehensive account of AI. Indeed, although it does touch on questions of performance, it is preoccupied largely with a relatively narrow range of popular AI techniques being used by some architects to generate some extraordinary design work at the moment. It therefore privileges the aesthetic potential of AI to produce visually stimulating images over performance-based considerations. This is where AI is arguably having its most significant impact at the moment. In the future, however, the success of AI is likely to be judged in a very different way: by its capacity to calculate the most efficient solution to a design challenge from the perspective of performance.

Chapter 1, 'What is AI?', is the most technical chapter. It introduces the basic principles of AI. It makes a series important distinctions between the different forms of AI and offers definitions of a number of key terms. It addresses the development of deep learning and the use of neural networks, and focuses in particular on a series of techniques used for generating images using DeepDream and various kinds of generative adversarial networks (GANs). The chapter then goes on to look at some of the AI techniques that have been developed for architecture, and the burgeoning field of 'architectural intelligence'.

Chapter 2, 'The history of AI', is more historical in its orientation. It offers a background history of AI, focusing in particular on the visibility and invisibility of AI. It introduces some of the important figures in the history of AI, such as Alan Turing, whose once secret and little-known contributions to computation have now been recognised and celebrated in popular culture. It highlights both the low points in its history – the so-called AI 'winters' – but also the high-profile media events – Chess, Jeopardy! and Go challenges – that have brought AI to worldwide attention. The chapter ends, however, with a warning about the risks of AI being exploited as a marketing tool, precisely because of its invisibility.

Chapter 3, 'AI, art and creativity', examines the capacity for AI to be 'creative'. It looks at the impact of generative AI techniques on the field of art, especially at a moment when AI artworks have not only been displayed at art exhibitions and sold at auctions, but have also won international art prizes. But this chapter also asks some searching questions. Is AI generated art really art? Who owns the copyright of AI generated art? And is it not time to rethink our understanding of creativity in the light of AI? The chapter concludes with the observation that perhaps AI might be able to offer a mirror in which to understand human intelligence and creativity.

Chapter 4, 'AI, media art and neuroscience', asks whether machines are able to 'dream' or 'hallucinate'. It highlights the importance of the moment when Refik Anadol projected his machine hallucinations onto Frank Gehry's Walt Disney Concert Hall in LA, and compares these machine hallucinations with the theory of 'controlled hallucinations' developed recently in the field of neuroscience. The chapter goes on to consider what insights AI and neuroscience can offer us into the way that architects think and see the world. The chapter concludes with the observation that the primary role of AI is perhaps to act as an inspirational muse for architects.

Chapter 5, 'AI and architecture', looks at the recent explosion of interest in AI within architectural design circles. It reflects upon the significance of the first ever exhibition of AI and architecture, and considers how AI is beginning to bring fresh approaches to architectural design. In particular, the chapter focuses on the different approaches that progressive architects, such as Wolf Prix (Coop Himmelb(l)au), Thom Mayne (Morphosis) and Patrik Schumacher (ZHA), are taking towards AI in their design practices. The chapter also considers what potential role AI might play in the fabrication of buildings.

Chapter 6, 'The future of the architectural office', considers how the architectural office of the future will engage with AI. Here the focus is less on experimentation and more on practical applications, less on aesthetics and more on questions of performance. The chapter engages with two of the leading developers of AI-based architectural software, Xkool and Spacemaker AI, and compares their different approaches. It argues that in terms of the introduction of AI into the architectural office, the crucial turning point will come when clients start to insist that their architects use AI. The chapter concludes by noting that in the age of AI, design itself will be reconfigured as a process of searching for potential outcomes rather than as the top-down form-making process that it has been in the past.

Chapter 7, 'AI and the city of the future', speculates on the potential impact of AI on the future of our cities. It argues that the key driver of change is less likely to be the quest for novel architectural forms, than the introduction of AI-based informational technologies. AI will begin to inform not only how cities are designed but also how they operate. Cities will become informational cities, and AI will operate as a form of 'brain' to allow them to operate more efficiently. The city of the future will become an intelligent, efficient city – a 'Brain City', an AI-enhanced version of the city of today.

The final chapter, 'The future of AI', speculates about the future of AI, and offers an overview of predictions made about the potential of AI. Will AI ever be able to match or even surpass human intelligence? Might it be able to achieve consciousness and think like us? And if so, what might be the consequences? The book concludes with a list of predictions about the impact of AI on the profession of architecture. It argues that over time AI will become an increasingly pervasive, indispensable tool in the architectural office, until eventually it will be capable of designing buildings on its own, and the full potential of AI will have been realised.

Intended audience

This book is aimed primarily, but not exclusively, at a younger generation – especially students of architecture. After all, this is the generation that can relate most to AI, because AI is already so much part of their world. This is the Facebook generation whose social lives depend upon AI, a generation that uses TikTok, Spotify and Wayz, and a generation that has absorbed AI into almost every aspect of their existence. Moreover, this is a generation for whom the real contributions of AI will kick in as they approach the peak of their careers. However, this book is also aimed at architects already in practice, offering them some insights into the kinds of tools that are now being developed, and into the changes that are likely to occur in architectural practice in the future. Finally, it is also aimed at the general public and anyone else interested in the creative potential of AI.

This is a timely book. AI is a hot topic. And new ideas, new design techniques, are being developed every day. Soon this book will need to be revised – updated – just as our technical devices are themselves constantly being updated. But at least it is a start. And perhaps its greatest contribution will be to help to initiate a debate about the potential impact of AI on the world of architecture. And, for sure, it will produce a counter-reaction. Many will be deeply sceptical of AI.

This series, however, anticipates this counter-reaction. This first volume is largely positive about AI, and argues that AI will eventually be able to design buildings. The second volume, however, looks at the dark side of AI. Among other concerns, it argues that inevitably AI will lead to the death of architecture, a profession that is already struggling.

Future generations, no doubt, will look back at this publication and see it as offering a time capsule of important ideas from a precise moment in time at the beginning of the third decade of the twenty-first century, when architectural culture began to embrace the possibilities afforded by AI.

1

What is AI?

A common definition of AI is that it seeks to mimic or simulate the intelligence of the human mind. As Margaret Boden puts it, 'AI seeks to make computers do the sorts of things that minds can do.'[1] Meanwhile John Kelleher describes AI as 'that field of research that is focused on developing computational systems that can perform tasks and activities normally considered to require human intelligence'.[2] The implication here is that AI might soon be able to take over these tasks and activities.[3]

In the longer term, however, AI is likely to exceed the intelligence of the human mind.[4] Human intelligence does not constitute the absolute pinnacle of intelligence. It merely constitutes 'human-level intelligence'. After all, there are already specific domains, such as the games of Chess and Go, where AI outperforms human intelligence. In the future, there are likely to be forms of intelligence that far exceed the intelligence of the human mind. Alternatively, then, we could define research into AI as an attempt to understand intelligence itself.

Typically the tasks performed by AI involve learning and problem-solving. But not all these tasks require intelligence.[5] Some, for example, merely involve vision or speech recognition. Importantly, however, as Boden notes, they all relate to our cognitive abilities: 'All involve psychological skills – such as perception, association, prediction, planning, motor control – that enable humans and animals to attain their goals.'[6] Thus, although some of the operations included in research into AI are not intelligent in themselves, they must nonetheless be included in any purview of AI, as they are crucial 'characteristics or behaviours' in the field of AI.[7]

When defining AI, it is necessary to draw up a series of distinctions. First and foremost, although the term 'intelligence' is used for both human beings and machines, we must be careful to distinguish AI from human intelligence. For the moment, at any rate, AI does not possess consciousness.[8] This is important to recognise. For example, AI might be capable of beating humans at a game of Chess or Go, but this does not mean that AI is *aware* that it is playing a game of Chess or Go.

At present, then, we are still limited to a relatively modest realm of AI that is known as 'narrow AI', which – as its name implies – is narrow and circumscribed in its potential.[9] 'Narrow AI' – also known as 'weak AI' – needs to be distinguished from 'strong AI' or artificial general intelligence (AGI), which is AI with consciousness. At the moment, AGI remains a long way off. The only 'examples' of AGI at the moment are pure fiction, such as characters from the world of the cinema, like Agent Smith in *The Matrix* or Ava in *Ex Machina*.[10] Nonetheless some philosophers, such as David Chalmers, think that development of GPT-3 by Open AI has brought the possibility of AGI much closer.[11]

Classic examples of 'narrow AI' would be Siri, Alexa, Cortona or any other form of AI assistant. However sophisticated these assistants might appear, they are operating within a limited range of predetermined functions. They cannot think for themselves any more than a pocket calculator can think, and are incapable of undertaking any activity that requires consciousness.[12]

The different forms of AI

The term AI is often used as though it is a singular, homogeneous category. Indeed, this is how the general public understands the term. However, there are in fact many different forms of AI, and even these can be further divided into a series of sub-categories. In order to understand AI, then, we need to differentiate the various forms of AI.

Within 'narrow AI' we should make a further distinction between the broader category of AI itself, 'machine learning' and 'deep learning'. These three can be seen to be nested within each other – somewhat like a series of Russian dolls, or layers in an onion – in that 'deep learning' is part of 'machine learning' that is itself part of AI. Early versions of AI referred to machines that had to be *programmed*

Evolutionaries put their trust in genetic programming that improves over successive generations much like natural selection itself.[26] Bayesians believe in the principle of probabilistic inference to overcome the problem of noise and incomplete information.[27] Analogisers subscribe to the logic of analogy and use that logic to recognise and learn from similarities.[28] However, the most significant 'tribes' in terms of the history of AI in general are the symbolists and the connectionists.

Symbolists believe in solving problems through inverse deduction, by using existing knowledge and identifying what further knowledge might be needed to make a deduction: 'For symbolists, all intelligence can be reduced to manipulating symbols, in the same way that a mathematician solves equations by replacing expressions by other expressions.'[29]

Connectionists, meanwhile, attempt to reverse engineer what the brain does through a process of backpropagation, so as to align a system's output with the desired response.[30] As Domingos observes, 'For connectionists, learning is what the brain does, and so what we need to do is to reverse engineer it. The brain learns by adjusting the strengths of connections between neurons, and the crucial problem is figuring out which connections are to blame for which errors and changing them accordingly.'[31] Not surprisingly, then, it is connectionism that would seem to offer us the best insights into how the human brain works.

For someone from outside the field, it might seem curious that there could be such a multiplicity of different approaches. And yet there has always been one dominant approach. For many years it was symbolism, but with the development of more sophisticated forms of neural networks and the emergence of deep learning, connectionism has now asserted itself as the dominant paradigm.[32]

Neural networks

Neural networks are composed of information processing units that are called 'neurons', and connections that control the flow of information between these units that are called 'synapses'.[33] Ethem Alpaydin defines the neural network as '[a] model composed of a network of simple units called neurons and connections between neurons called synapses. Each synapse has a direction and a weight, and the weight defines the effect of the neuron before on the neuron after.'[34]

The neural networks used in connectionist AI should be distinguished from the virtual machines used in symbolic AI. They operate in parallel, are self-organising and can work without expert knowledge of task or domain. As Boden puts it, 'Sequential instructions are replaced by massive parallelism, top-down control by bottom-up processing, and logic by probability.'[35] They need to be trained by being fed a series of input–output pairs as training examples. The system then 'learns' over a period of time and tries to find the optimal weighting for each connection, so that when fed an input the output matches – as far as possible – the training examples. Nonetheless, they are robust, good at discerning patterns – even when incomplete – and can deal with 'messy' evidence.[36] Think of how you can continue a tune, based only on the first few notes.

The simplest way for a neural network to process an image is to operate in one direction, known as 'feed forward'. A network consists of an 'input layer', an 'output layer' and – in between – multiple internal layers known as 'hidden layers'. Each layer consists of simulated neurons. These neurons each 'compute' their input based on the 'weight' of the input's connection, applying a threshold value to determine its 'activation value'. In so doing, each neuron extracts

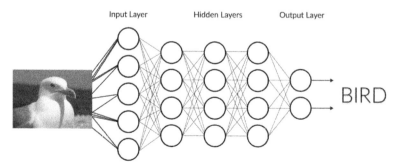

FIGURE 1.2 Diagram of a neural network. A neural network processes an image in feed forward direction with its behaviour characterised by the strengths of the synapses between the layers of neurons.

and filters out certain 'features', before passing on its activation value to neurons in the next layer.[37] Each subsequent layer computes progressively higher level features, until a classification output is generated based on its probability of being correct.[38]

Neural networks are named after the neurons in the human brain. However, although certain comparisons can be drawn between neural networks and the brain, a clear distinction should be made between the 'neurons' in neural networks and the neurons in the brain. Certainly neural networks are nowhere near as sophisticated as the human brain. Multiple as the layers of neural networks are in deep learning, they are not as numerous as the countless networks in the human brain.[39] Neural networks are therefore not so much modelled on the human brain, as *inspired* by it. As Yoshua Bengio comments, 'While machine learning is trying to put knowledge into computers by allowing computers to learn from examples, deep learning is doing it in a way that is inspired by the brain.'[40]

Melanie Mitchell prefers to use the term 'unit' rather than 'neuron', since a simulated neuron bears so little resemblance to an actual neuron in the brain. Mitchell sums up the process as follows:

To process an image . . . the network performs its computation layer by layer, from left to right. Each hidden unit computes its activation value; these activation values then become the inputs for the output units, which then compute their own activations . . . The activation of an output unit can be thought of as the network's confidence that it is 'seeing' the corresponding digit; the digit category with the highest confidence can be taken as the network's answer – its classification.[41]

Backpropagation

Deep learning depends on 'backpropagation' – sometimes called 'backprop'. This allows a neural network to effectively operate in reverse in order to correct earlier prediction errors. Backpropagation refers to a process whereby information about the prediction error propagates backwards through the various layers of the neural network, allowing the original 'weights' to be recalibrated and updated, so that the system can 'converge' or edge closer to the correct answer, in a manner not so dissimilar to reverse engineering. With deep learning this process is improved by increasing the number of hidden layers. Indeed, there can be anything from four layers to over 1,000 layers – hence the term 'deep' in deep learning.[42]

Each individual cycle through the full training dataset, whereby the weights are recalibrated, is referred to as an 'epoch' of training. Typically many epochs are required, sometimes up to several thousand, and in principle the more epochs, the better the results, although there is no absolute guarantee that the results will continue to improve.

Convolutional neural networks

There are several different types of neural networks. With deep learning, convolutional neural networks (ConvNets) have become increasingly popular, especially for classifying images.[43] The term 'convolution' refers to the calculation performed by each layer based on the preceding layer.[44] This process vastly improves the process of classifying images, so much so that ConvNets have become all but universal.

ConvNets are modelled on the visual cortex of the human brain. Neuroscientists David Hubel and Torsten Weisel observe that the brain has various layers of neurons in the visual cortex that act as 'detectors' operating in a hierarchy looking for increasingly complex features. These layers operate in both a feed-forward and a feed-backwards way, suggesting that our perception is influenced strongly by prior knowledge and expectations.[45]

ConvNets behave in a similar way to standard neural networks, but have activation maps – based on the detectors in the brain – operating layer by layer, detecting features such as edges, depending on their orientation.[46] By the time the final layer is reached, the ConvNet has detected some relatively complex features, based on the dataset on which it has been trained. At this point, a classification module, consisting of a traditional neural network, is deployed to evaluate the network's confidence – in percentage terms – that it has recognised the image. Mitchell offers a helpful summary of this highly complex process:

Inspired by Hubel and Weisel's findings on the brain's visual cortex, ConvNet takes an input image and transforms it – via convolutions – into a set of activation maps with increasingly complex features. The features at the highest convolutional layer are fed into a traditional neural network, which outputs confidence percentages for the network's known object categories. The object with the highest confidence is returned as the network's classification of the image.

Image classification – or 'discriminative modelling' – has become an important application of AI, especially in the domains of self-driving cars and facial recognition systems. From an architectural perspective, however, an even more significant consequence of image classification is the possibility that it affords for the generation of images or 'image synthesis' – a challenge long considered the holy grail by AI researchers.

DeepDream

Image synthesis is a category within deep learning.[47] One of the earliest methods of image synthesis is DeepDream, a computer vision programme developed by Alex Mordvintsev of Google Artists and Machine Intelligence (AMI) and released in 2015.[48] Typically ConvNets are used for recognising images. With DeepDream, however, it is possible to generate images by reversing the flow of information, sometimes referred to as 'inverting the network'. Instead of recognising an image and categorising it, DeepDream can be used to start with a category and proceeds to generate an image.[49] For example, whereas a standard neural network can recognise an image of a cat, and categorise it as a 'cat', DeepDream is able to start with the category 'cat' and generate an image that resembles a cat.[50] Instead of operating 'from image to media', then, DeepDream operates 'from media to image'.[51]

Importantly, although computational neural networks are trained to discriminate between images, they need to have some understanding of those images. And this is what allows them to also generate images, when operating in reverse.[52] However, DeepDream

FIGURE 1.3 Martin Thomas, *Aurelia Aurita*, DeepDream generated image (2015). DeepDream image generated after fifty iterations by a neural network trained to perceive dogs.

often produces a somewhat 'trippy' picture that appears vaguely surrealistic with a multiplicity of objects generated in a variety of poses.[53] It is also possible to produce an image by starting with an arbitrary image instead of 'noise' or a specific embedding, and allowing the network to analyse and optimise it.[54]

Generative adversarial networks

Currently the most popular technique of image synthesis among architects, however, is generative adversarial networks (GANs). These were first proposed by Ian Goodfellow in 2014, but have undergone rapid development in the intervening years.[55]

A GAN is a technique for training a computer to perform complex tasks through a generative process measured against a set of training images. It represents a major breakthrough in the quest to synthesise images and overcomes the problem of objects appearing in a variety of poses that compromises DeepDream. It also generates images with significantly better resolution.

A GAN is based on a competition between two different neural networks. It consists of a bottom-up generator – or 'artist' – that

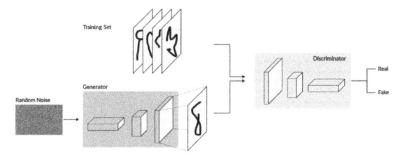

Training Set

Generator

Random Noise

Discriminator

Real

Fake

FIGURE 1.4 Diagram illustrating the workings of a generative adversarial network (GAN). One way to think of the operation of a GAN would be the contest between an art forger trying to produce a convincing work of art, and an art expert trying to ascertain whether or not the work is fake.

generates images, and a top-down discriminator – or 'critic' – that evaluates those images.[56] In the competition, the generator attempts to fool the discriminator by producing images so realistic that the discriminator would be unable to distinguish them from a real data set. Mishak Navak describes the process as follows:

> [A] Generator (an artist)generates an image. The Generator does not know anything about the real images and learns by interacting with the Discriminator. [The] discriminator (an art critic) determines whether an object is 'real' and 'fake' . . . The Generator keeps creating new images and refining its process until the Discriminator can no longer tell the difference between the generated images and the real training images.[57]

The two work in tandem and improve over time, so that the 'artist' trains the 'critic', and the 'critic' trains the 'artist'.[58] Once the 'artist' has been trained, the 'critic' can be removed.

The invention of GANs has since led to an extraordinary explosion of research and the development of many different versions, with their outputs becoming ever more refined.[59] GANs build upon the developments of DeepDream in interesting new ways.[60] And although they are not without their problems, the standard has improved substantially in the relatively few years since GANs were first developed.[61]

The Progressive Growing of GANs (ProGAN), for example, increases the resolution of the image, layer by layer.[62] This allows the whole process to speed up, producing far greater realism than previously achieved. However, there is limited control of certain features in the generated image, leading to problem of 'entanglement' whereby any slight tweak or amendment to one feature has a knock-on effect on the next.[63]

A StyleGAN offers further improvements in terms of resolution and quality, by starting with very low resolution images and gradually increasing the resolution.[64] It treats an image as a collection of different 'styles', whereby each 'style' controls the effect at a

FIGURE 1.5 StyleGANs, *Thispersondoesnotexist* (2019). This image is composed of four separate StyleGAN images of fictious people generated using the website www.thispersondoesnotexist.com.

FIGURE 1.7 Immanuel Koh, 3D Printed GAN Chair (2020). Deep generative adversarial networks (GANs) trained with 3D models of 10,000 chairs and 4,000 residential buildings are used to synthesise novel designs. Shown here is a 3D printed instance sampled from the shared latent features of chairs and buildings.

productive, and has shown that an unsupervised approach using point clouds can come close to matching the performance of supervised approaches.[84] Point clouds, however, consist of points and do not offer any surface as such.

Object meshes, meanwhile, have certain advantages over both voxels and meshes, in that they are more computationally efficient than voxels and offer more visual information than meshes. However, 3D meshes can cause a problem if they are of different sizes, in that most rendering engines are not differentiable.

At present a differential mesh renderer seems to be the most promising approach to operating in 3D. In 2020, PyTorch3D was launched: an open source library for 3D learning that overcomes many of the problems by using a differential neural mesh renderer to synthesise 3D forms. PyTorch3D makes it possible to edit objects based on DeepDream and style transfer technique.[85] Modelling in 3D, however, remains a challenging area, and one that still needs to be resolved.

ArchiGAN

From an architectural perspective, the main constraint with GANs is that they operate within the domain of 2D representation, whereas architecture consists of 3D form. Nonetheless, architectural drawings – plans, sections, elevations and even axonometric drawings and perspectives – are themselves 2D representations. It is therefore their capacity to generate images, as Stanislas Chaillou observes, that makes GANs so significant for architectural design:

> Goodfellow's research turns upside down the definition of AI, from an analytical tool to a generative agent. By the same token, he brings AI one step closer to architectural concerns: drawing and image production. All in all, from simple networks to GANs, a new generation of tools coupled with increasingly cheaper and accessible computational power is today positioning AI as an affordable and powerful medium.[86]

Chaillou is an architect, but unlike most architects who find themselves limited to tools developed by others, he has developed his own tools.[87] For his masters thesis at Harvard GSD, Chaillou designed ArchiGAN, a version of GANs that uses a Pix2Pix GAN-model to design floor plans for an entire building. By effectively nesting models of the furniture layout within a partitioned apartment, and then nesting the partitioned apartment within the overall building footprint, he is able to achieve a 'generation stack' where each of these three layers are interrelated. Importantly also, Chaillou allows the user to amend the design at each stage.

The first step is to establish a building footprint based on the site. This is done with a model trained to generate footprints based on Geographic Information System (GIS) data using Pix2Pix. The second step is to introduce partition walling and fenestration so as to generate the floor plan, with the position of the entrance and main windows specified by the user. A database of over 800 annotated plans is used as input, and as output the system generates a layout with rooms encoded with colours to specify a programme. The final step is to generate the furniture for each room based on its programme – a bed in the bedroom, a table in the dining room and so on. These models

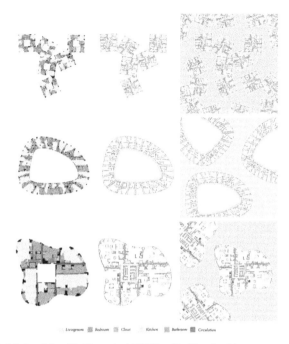

Livingroom Bedroom Closet Kitchen Bathroom Circulation

FIGURE 1.8 Stanislas Chaillou, ArchiGANs. Chaillou is able to generate stacked plans of buildings using ArchiGAN, a Pix2Pix version of GANs.

are 'chained' to each other, so that as the user intervenes and starts modifying the footprint, for example, the partition walling and furniture layout will adjust automatically.

There are, of course, limitations to this model. Firstly, if each floor is different, there is no way of guaranteeing that load-bearing walls on each floor will be aligned. It is therefore assumed that the external wall is load-bearing, although it is possible to introduce internal load-bearing walls. Secondly, the resolution of each drawing is currently too low, although it could be improved with more computing power. Finally, GANs can only handle pixel information, a format incompatible with standard computational tools in the architectural office.[88] Here we should not overlook graph-based neural networks and vector-based neural networks, which perform better than GANs and other image-based neural networks in certain specific tasks, especially when the architectural data can be represented as vectors (CAD drawings or parameters).

Beyond representation

It might be tempting to associate AI solely with the field of representation. After all, the datasets used for AI often consist of representational images, and the term 'style transfer' is often used, especially in connection with GANs.[89] It is important to recognise, however, that a GAN constitutes a process, albeit a process that operates with representational images. Moreover, we could argue that 'feature extraction' is a better term than 'style transfer'. We could also argue that a GAN in itself is unlikely to promote a particular style, if by 'style' we mean the idea of a predefined representational logic – an aesthetic 'template' – according to which the work is produced, for the simple reason that it cannot be controlled. Finally, although GANs – and image synthesis in general – are popular amongst those working in the visual realm, they constitute a relatively minor research field within machine vision, which is itself only one of the many categories within deep learning.[90]

AI, then, is certainly not limited to representational concerns. Indeed, as we shall see, performance-based concerns are likely to be the area in which AI will have its greatest impact, especially in terms of architectural practice and urban design. Indeed, at an urban scale, where data-driven and performance-informed design is becoming increasingly popular, representational considerations play only a minor role. Concerns about improving the material performance of buildings and reducing carbon emissions have now become paramount, and go beyond considerations of mere economic efficiencies to become an ethical imperative in a world of diminishing resources and global warming. As a result, the earlier obsession with form for the sake of form has given way to a more intelligent approach, whereby form is informed increasingly by performative concerns. Performance, of course, has long been a concern within the fields of architecture and urban design. However, with the introduction of advanced informational systems drawing upon satellite information and data mining, there are more opportunities to model and test the performance of designs with far greater accuracy.

One key area, where AI is being used increasingly for performance-driven design is structural design, where topological optimisation, an established GOFAI technique, is now being applied increasingly in

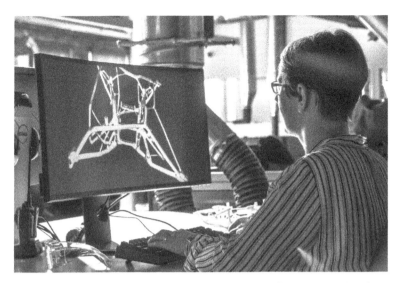

FIGURE 1.9 Autodesk DreamCatcher is a generative design system based on structural optimisation.

generative design. Examples would include Project Dreamcatcher, a generative design system developed by Autodesk, that allows designers to generate a range of designs by specifying goals and constraints, such as functions, materials, performance criteria and costs restrictions, allowing them to trade off different approaches and explore design solutions.[91] Another example would be Ameba, a bi-directional evolutionary structural optimisation (BESO) technology developed by Mike Xie of Xie Technologies.[92] And since Grasshopper and other algorithmic design techniques are considered basic forms of AI, plugins for Rhino and Grasshopper, such as Rhinovault, can also be considered as forms of AI.

Another key area where AI has proved very effective is in the environmentally sustainable design of new buildings.[93] It can also be deployed, however, in monitoring and controlling the energy use in existing buildings and for other more general environmental issues, such as thermal comfort, wind comfort, lighting levels, solar radiation, pedestrian traffic and sightlines.[94] Increasingly the environmental control of a building is being achieved through the use of a 'digital twin', a digital model that simulates the performance of a potential

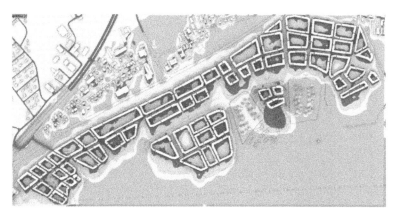

FIGURE 1.10 Theodoros Galanos, InFraRed Wind Comfort Study, Vienna, Austria (2020). InFraRed in action: real-time, mixed-initiative urban design based on quantifiable performance data. The pre-trained model is deployed in Grasshopper and coupled with an intuitive interface allowing for real-time visualisation of the designer's decisions on performance.

or actual building.[95] Digital models, of course, have been around for some time, but a digital twin is a relatively new invention.[96] A digital twin is a digital model that is constantly being updated with real-time information from both the Internet of Things (IoT), and direct sensors.[97] As Michael Batty defines it, 'A digital twin is a mirror image of a physical process that is articulated alongside the process in question, usually matching exactly the operation of the physical process which takes place in real time.'[98] A digital twin can be used both for analyzing performance in the past and for predicting performance in the future. And it can operate at a range of scales from a building scale, where it can be used, for example, to model the behaviour of occupants, through to an urban scale, where it can be used, as we shall see, to monitor and control traffic flow.[99]

In recent years the range of AI assisted and AI driven applications has exploded. Here we might cite the proliferation of generative design and topological optimisation products, such as ANSYS Discovery AIM, Bentley Generative Components, Comsol Optimisation Module, Siemens Solid Edge Generative Design, and many others.[100] The only area that remains as yet underdeveloped is the application of machine learning to tools for architecture, construction and engineering (ACE).

There are signs, however, that change is afoot, with the Austrian Institute of Technology, for example, producing a number of machine

'The future of architecture will be intelligent.'

learning tools, such as daylightGAN, ArchElites and InFraRed.[101] In fact, it is difficult to imagine an area where machine learning will not be used in the future. AI will undoubtedly make a number of significance contributions to architectural culture. It will allow us to design more efficiently, generate a broader range of designs, test out our designs in simulation, and control the performance of buildings once constructed.

The future of architecture will be intelligent.

branches; cybernetics and symbolic computing.[24] 'Those interested in *life*,' notes Boden, 'stayed in cybernetics, and those interested in the *mind* turned to symbolic computing.'[25]

If, however, we were to isolate one particular event that was instrumental in not only cementing this divide, but also in defining the term 'AI', it would surely be the Dartmouth Summer Workshop on Artificial Intelligence held in 1956.[26] The event was proposed by John McCarthy, Marvin Minsky, Nathanial Rochester and Claude Shannon, and was attended by many of the figures who would later become luminaries in the field of AI:

> We propose that a 2 month, 10 man study of artificial intelligence be carried out during the summer of 1956 at Dartmouth College in Hanover, New Hampshire. The study is to proceed on the basis of the conjecture that every aspect of learning or any other feature of intelligence can in principle be so precisely described that a machine can be made to simulate it. An attempt will be made to find how to make machines use language, form abstractions and concepts, solve kinds of problems now reserved for humans, and improve themselves. We think that a significant advance can be made in one or more of these problems if a carefully selected group of scientists work on it together for a summer.[27]

The event not only helped to define the field, but also led to the adoption of the term 'artificial intelligence', even though McCarthy himself was not fully comfortable with it.[28]

What followed was a period of euphoria and intense, well-funded research, fuelled by heady speculation. Indeed in 1967, Minsky claimed that within a generation the problem of artificial intelligence would be solved.[29] All of a sudden, AI came into the spotlight. With time, however, it became clear that these aspirations were unrealistic. For this and other reasons, funding dried up and the first 'AI winter' occurred.

AI winters

AI winters could be defined as periods in which confidence in the potential of AI collapsed on the part of venture capitalists and government funding agencies. These crises of confidence were triggered initially by reports from within the academic community, but ultimately owe their origins to overinflated expectations – much like the dot.com boom and bust in the 1990s – and illustrated the volatility of public confidence in the new technology. The first AI winter occurred around 1974 and was prompted largely by two setbacks.

One of the setbacks was that, despite huge investment by the US government in developing instantaneous translation as part of its Cold War effort, the results did not live up to the hype. AI was quite capable of translating words, but only if in the correct order.[30] There were also other problems that led to humorous outcomes, such as 'out of sight, out of mind' being translated as 'an invisible lunatic', or 'the spirit is willing but the flesh is weak' as 'the vodka is good but the meat is rotten'.[31] As a result, the primary source of military funding in the United States, the Defense Advanced Research Projects Agency (DARPA), withdrew its funding from a major machine learning research project. Meanwhile in 1973, Professor James Lighthill issued a controversial report in the United Kingdom, where he noted that AI had failed to live up to its somewhat grandiose aspirations.[32] The net result was a sudden loss of confidence in AI, leading to a drastic reduction in funding for AI research – a phenomenon which then rippled throughout the rest of Europe.

The other setback was that confidence began to fade in connectionist AI and the potential of neural networks, stemming from the early work of McCulloch and Pitts. This was partly the result of the publication of the book *Perceptrons: An Introduction to Computational Geometry*, written Marvin Minsky and Seymour Papert, who were enthusiasts of symbolic AI.[33] The book outlined the limitations of the connectionist approach that relied on the use of the perceptron, an algorithm for supervised learning, invented by Frank Rosenblatt in 1958.[34] Rosenblatt had predicted that the perceptron would also be able to make decisions and even translate languages.[35] Indeed, the perceptron did show some promise, and, as became clear later when deep learning was developed, connectionist AI is quite capable of both making decisions and translating languages.

The publication of *Perceptrons* marked one of the most controversial episodes in the history of AI. For the most part, competition between the various 'tribes' in the AI community took more than 3,000 years ago and remains hugely popular there. The Chinese nation was clearly transfixed by the match. There was an estimated worldwide television audience of 280 million for this event, a significant proportion of which was in China.[79] And the victory of AlphaGo over Lee sent a seismic shock through the whole nation. The impact of the match on China should not be understated. It was a huge wake up call for them. As Lee notes, 'Overnight, China plunged into an artificial intelligence fever.'[80] In what has been described by Kai-Fu Lee as China's 'Sputnik Moment', the Chinese government realised after the match that it was lagging behind the West in a technology that held vast potential.[81] The original 'sputnik moment' was, of course, the moment when the United States was jolted into action in the Space Race, after being seriously embarrassed by the success of the Soviet Union in launching a satellite into space.[82]

The Chinese government promptly decided to initiate an ambitious and rapid programme of investment in AI.[83] On 18 October 2017 – a year and a half after the match – Chinese President Xi Jinping announced a new plan for China to invest in AI with a view to overtaking the US in AI development by 2030.[84] Kai Fu-Lee astutely observes, 'If AlphaGo was China's Sputnik moment, the government's AI plan was like President John F. Kennedy's landmark speech calling for America to land a man on the moon.'[85] In fact some have argued that China has already surpassed the US, if judged on the basis of the number of articles published on AI, and looks set to claim the top spot for most cited papers by 2025.[86]

If, then, the original Sputnik moment in the States led to the Space Race that was itself a manifestation of the Cold War, would not the second Sputnik moment in China lead to the AI race, which is itself a new form of Cold War? 'No,' says Lee, 'this is not a new Cold War.'[87] Although AI can be used for military purposes, its true value lies in opening up to a new technology that will surely benefit the whole of humanity. Instead of the Cold War, the comparison should be with the Industrial Revolution or the invention of electricity. But it most certainly was, as Lee so aptly observes, both a 'game' and a 'game changer', at least as far as China was concerned.[88]

The match also had a significant impact on AI funding in South Korea. On 17 March – just two days after the contest – the South

Korean government pledged 1 trillion won ($863 million) for research in AI over the next five years. South Korean President Park Geun-Hye expressed her gratitude for the match: 'Above all, Korean society is ironically lucky, that thanks to the "AlphaGo shock", we have learned the importance of AI before it is too late.'[89]

AI and visibility

The history of AI can be read as a history of visibility and invisibility. Most people are largely unaware of AI, and have little understanding of what it does. And often even those who do understand what it actually does, do not understand quite how it does it – as in the case of deep learning.

Such is the low profile of AI that it takes a high profile event to bring it to our attention. This could be a news headline comment by a famous figure, such as Stephen Hawking or Elon Musk. Or it could be a competition staged on television. It is these moments of great visibility that really capture the public imagination. The match between Lee and AlphaGo was not only watched by a vast TV audience, but also became the subject of an award-winning documentary, *AlphaGo*.[90] By comparison, almost no one has heard of the subsequent match between AlphaGo Master and Ke Jie, the actual world champion. This second event was not promoted in the media in quite the same way.[91] In fact, perhaps the most spectacular achievement of all is that of the development of AlphaZero, a programme that trained itself entirely using reinforcement learning – an extraordinary feat that that has passed by largely unnoticed. In short, AI has gone largely unnoticed by most people, except for a series of high-profile moments.

Just as AI itself is invisible, so research on AI passes largely unnoticed by the general public. In some cases this is because there can be sound business reasons not to divulge information about research that is still ongoing. However, in most cases the 'invisibility' of research into AI is simply down to the fact that it is either not sufficiently interesting or accessible to the general public to be covered by the press. From the perspective of the media, an event is not an event unless it is newsworthy. Likewise, from the perspective of the general public, an event is not an event unless it is covered by the media. The same principle applies to the many people beavering away behind the scenes who have helped to make AI what it is today. Visibility is everything.

These high-profile events might be entertaining, but the real intention behind them is to showcase AI and raise awareness of its commercial potential, so as to impress would-be financial backers. In so doing the invisible logic of AI is made visible. It is simply a question of marketing. Nor should we forget that – in terms of marketing – AI itself is working invisibly 'behind the scenes', feeding us advertisements for products that our previous search record suggests that we might find appealing. Advertising by stealth.

Potentially more disconcerting, however, is the opposite tendency of using AI for branding purposes, even when little or no AI is actually being used. For example, Hansen Electronics has been marketing a humanoid robot, Sophia, with some success. Sophia not only looks human – much like the replicants in *Blade Runner*, also an artificial life form – but is also presented as though 'she' thinks like humans. In October 2017, Sophia became the first robot to be made a citizen of Saudi Arabia.[92] And in November 2017 'she' became the first robot to be named 'Innovation Champion' by the United Nations Development

FIGURE 2.5 Sophia, the humanoid robot produced by Hanson Robotics, is photographed here in the 'AI for Good' Global Summit in Geneva on 7 June 2017. Photo: Fabrice Coffrini, Getty (693354896).

programme.[93] Sophia has been marketed as though it is a conscious, sentient being. But in fact Sophia is anything but conscious, and has been decried by the AI community. For Rodney Brooks, Sophia is 'completely bogus and a total sham', while for Benedict Evans, Sophia is little more than 'a tape recorder with a rubber head on it'.[94] Few would be fooled into believing that Sophia is a human being.[95] But this is not the issue here. While the Turing Test is designed to test whether a computer can successfully masquerade as a sentient human, Sophia is an automaton masquerading as AGI – a sentient robot. And the purpose of this masquerade is to impress the general public and to promote Hansen Electronics. Never underestimate the power of AI to excite the general public. As Maria Dantz of Spacemaker AI comments, 'AI is certainly something that opens doors, because people want to hear about it.'[96]

Likewise – despite its name – the architectural practice AI SpaceFactory does not actually use AI in any of its design and fabrication processes at the time of writing, even though it has plans to do so in the future.[97] While AI can be very good at detecting spam and other forms of marketing, it can also be exploited in marketing. Should we not be suspicious of any company with AI in its name?

This is the logic of 'inverse camouflage'. If the logic of camouflage is to pretend something is not there when it is – making the visible invisible – the logic of inverse camouflage is to pretend that something is there when it is not. It is a question of making the visible invisible, versus making the invisible visible. But could inverse camouflage not be a cunning marketing strategy – 'marketing the invisible'? Who is to know whether AI is being used or not? Might these companies pass their own inverse Turing Test by persuading the general public that they are using AI when they are not? In the age of AI, what is AI but the ultimate marketing opportunity?

Beware the AI of marketing![98]

3

AI, art and creativity

As the daughter of the poet Lord Byron, Ada Lovelace was no stranger to creativity. She describes the Analytical Engine proposed by Charles Babbage in highly poetic terms: 'The analytical engine weaves algebraic patterns, just as the Jacquard loom weaves flowers and leaves.'[1] In fact Lovelace believed that the Analytical Engine would even be capable of composing music. She notes, 'Supposing, for instance, that the fundamental relations of pitched sounds in the science of harmony and of musical composition were susceptible of such expression and adaptations, the engine might compose elaborate and scientific pieces of music of any degree of complexity or extent.'[2] However, Lovelace added that the Analytical Engine could only do what it was programmed to do: 'The Analytical Machine has no pretensions whatsoever to originate anything. It can do whatever we know how to order it to perform. It can follow analysis, but it has no power of anticipating any analytical revelation of truths. Its province is to assist us in making available what we are already acquainted with.'[3] Her point here is that a machine, such as the Analytical Engine, would be incapable of originating anything. Any creativity would have to come from the programmer.[4] But is this really the case?

Turing begins his famous article, 'Computing Machinery and Intelligence', with the question, 'Can Machines Think?'[5] In fact Turing speculates that eventually machines should be able to do anything that a human can do, to the point that they should be able to write sonnets:

We have to have some experience with the machine before we really know its capabilities. It may take years before we settle down to the new possibilities, but I do not see why it should not enter any one of the fields normally covered by the human intellect, and eventually compete on equal terms. I do not think that you can even draw the line about sonnets.[6]

Turing is confident, however, that machines can *learn*. Before machine learning had even been contemplated, Turing speculated on the possibility of machines learning, correctly surmising that we might not know how the process happens: 'An important feature of a learning machine is that its teacher will often be very largely ignorant of what is going on inside.'[7] Indeed, as Turing also notes, machines can produce surprising results: 'Machines take me by surprise with great frequency.'[8]

Computers can also produce novelty, as Richard and Daniel Susskind observe, 'Contrary to widespread belief, machines are now capable of generating novel outcomes, entirely beyond the contemplation of their original human designers.'[9] Clearly computers can learn, be innovative and even perhaps compose sonnets. But can they be genuinely creative?

The general consensus would seem to hold that computers cannot be genuinely creative, and creativity is often cited as one of the realms where AI is relatively weak. Such criticism echoes the argument of Lovelace, that computers can only do what they were programmed to do. They cannot initiate anything. Much depends, however, on how we understand creativity. Can we say that a computer is creative, for example, when it has no consciousness, and does not even 'realise' that it is being creative? When it comes to generating art, Melanie Mitchell goes further and argues that it is also important to be able to *appreciate* the art that has been produced, and this is not something that AI – for the moment, at any rate – is able to do, as AI does not have consciousness.[10] As such, Mitchell does not believe that AI can be creative.[11]

For sure, it is clear that AI is capable of *generating* novel outputs. It is also capable of recognising patterns and extrapolating further material based on those patterns. But can AI also produce art?[12]

A brief history of AI art

There is an interesting comparison to be made between traditional patrons of art and contemporary tech companies. In the past, institutions such as the Church or established banking families, such as the Medici family in Florence, Italy, supported and sponsored artists and sculptors, like Michelangelo. In the present, however, tech companies, such as Amazon, Microsoft, Apple and Google, increasingly play that role. It is a role that should not be underestimated.

Recently, Blaise Agüera y Arcas, a software engineer with an interest in machine vision, set up a group within Google, Artists and Machine Intelligence (AMI), that explores the potential applications of machine intelligence within the realm of art. Arcas asks:

> What do art and technology have to do with each other? What is machine intelligence, and what does 'machine intelligence art' look, sound and feel like? What are the emerging relationships between humans and machines; what does it mean to be human; and what can we learn about intelligence, human or otherwise, through art? How should we think about our future?[13]

In March 2018, Google AMI held an exhibition in San Francisco in collaboration with the Gray Area Foundation. The exhibition was of DeepDream generated art, and was quite possibly the first ever exhibition of AI generated art. In his opening address, Arcas was keen to emphasise that this was not an experiment to explore whether DeepDream would be accepted by the art community.[14] He was more confident than that: 'We believe machine intelligence is an innovation that will profoundly affect art.'[15] AI is proving an increasingly popular medium for artists, even though there is still significant resistance to it within more conservative art circles.[16]

Then, later in 2018, *Edmond de Belamy*, a portrait generated by the Paris-based art collective Obvious, using Creative Adversarial Networks (CANs), was auctioned at Christie's for the remarkable sum of $432,500, almost forty-five times the initial estimate, becoming the first AI-generated artwork to be sold at auction.[17] This caused outrage among some, not because it was an artwork generated by AI, but rather because Obvious had not written the training algorithms or the data set.[18] They had simply tweaked algorithms available on an open course website, and exploited the results.

Significantly, it has been found that human beings are incapable of distinguishing artworks created by CANs from artworks created by

FIGURE 3.1 Obvious, *Edmond de Belamy* (2018). Edmond de Belamy was generated by a neural network by the Paris-based arts-collective, Obvious, and became the first such artwork to be auctioned, when it was sold at Christie's for $432,500 on 25 October 2018.

artists. As such, it would appear that CANs are capable of passing the Turing Test. But is this not the very purpose of GANs themselves? If the intention of the generator/artist in a GAN is to produce an image that a discriminator/critic would think is real, is that not precisely what CAN is doing in generating an artwork? In effect we have the Turing Test being played out every time that a GAN – of whatever kind – is initiated. Whereas the Turing Test is about fooling the judge, a GAN is about fooling the art critic. Perhaps the only real difference between what happens with the Turing Test and a GAN is that the GAN can learn from its mistakes and improve its performance until such time as it succeeds, whereas in the Turing Test there is no opportunity for the machine to improve and be reappraised.[19]

Another landmark in terms of the impact of AI on the world of art was reached that same year (2018), when Mario Klingemann was awarded the Lumen Prize Gold Award for his work, *The Butcher's Son*, also generated using GANs.[20] This is the first time that a major international art prize has been awarded to an artwork generated by a machine. As Klingemann notes:

FIGURE 3.2 Ahmed Eigammel, *Ich bin ein Berliner* (2017). Ahmed Eigammel is the founder and director of the Art and Artificial Intelligence Laboratory at Rutgers University, and uses his creative adversarial network to generate artworks.

This image has been generated entirely by a machine using a chain of GANs. In this chain a randomly generated stick-figure is used as an input to the first GAN, which produces a painterly-looking low-resolution proto-image. In several steps, the low resolution image is 'transhanced' and upscaled by another GAN increasing the resolution and adding details and textures. I control this process indirectly by training the model on selected data sets, the model's hyperparameters and eventually by making a curatorial choice, by picking among the thousands of variations produced by the models the one that speaks to me most.[21]

The following year, in 2019, the first ever solo exhibition for AI art took place in the HG Contemporary gallery in Chelsea, New York. The 'artist' was Ahmed Elgammal, a computer scientist and the developer of CANs. Elgammal has now established his own art and artificial intelligence laboratory to produce art through a process he now calls AICAN.[22] AI scientists, it would seem, are now more street savvy and willing to cash in on the possibilities afforded by their inventions. As Bogost puts it, 'The AI-art gold rush is here.'[23]

FIGURE 3.3 GauGAN, named after the painter Paul Gauguin, is able to generate a photorealistic image from a simple sketch, using a style transfer algorithm.

Who needs Gauguin?

GauGAN is a real time AI art application developed by Nvidia that synthesises photorealistic images from diagrammatic sketches.[24] As its name implies, it evokes the potential of Paul Gauguin, the French Impressionist painter, to create paintings that can now be simulated by style transfer techniques. But what makes GauGAN so special is that it can create photorealistic landscape images from crude initial brush strokes in real time. It is trained on over a million actual landscape images.

GauGAN has been lauded within the AI community and received two major awards, 'Best of Show' and 'Audience Choice', at SIGRRAPH 2019.[25] The programme is undeniably impressive and highly sophisticated from a technical perspective, but its potential applications within the world of art are unclear. Nvidia researcher, Gavril Klimov, who was part of the development team, tries to sell its virtues: 'As an artist it's extremely valuable to be able to generate content quickly because artists need to iterate fast. GauGAN allows us to generate our ideas at a speed that was previously not possible, and this will become a main tool for artists to use in the future.'[26] The point here is that the results are so astonishingly photorealistic that they undercut precisely the contribution that artists hitherto have been able to make. The question is not so much, 'Why spend months on a painting, when you can generate one in real time?' as, 'Who needs Gauguin, when you have GauGAN?'

Surely those to whom it would appeal most would be non-artists, or at least those incapable of painting like Gauguin. In some senses, one might even argue that GauGAN might be best suited to those interested in producing fakes, given the history of the production of fake paintings within the art world. Of course, in the hands of the right artist, such a technique might be open to extraordinary inventive potential as a prosthetic extension of the artistic imagination. Here I am not referring to the simple primary applications envisioned by the developers of GauGAN, so much as a range of as yet unimagined open secondary applications invented by the artistic community.[27] Nonetheless, the question remains as to whether true artists would ever want to use such a tool, at least in the straightforward manner that immediately presents itself. It would seem highly unlikely that an art-generating product would appeal to artists themselves. Who needs GauGAN, when you have Gauguins?

But who is the author?

From a technical perspective it is clearly possible to use AI to generate artworks of a high enough standard to win major art prizes, and be auctioned at some of the world's most important auction houses. At the same time, the introduction of AI-generated artworks provokes a number of interesting challenges for the art world. The incursion of AI into the art world echoes the invention of photography. In many ways, the challenge that photography made to painting – and the outcry that it caused – offers an interesting parallel to the challenge that AI now poses to art. Arcas refers to this, and predicts that some will reject the possibility of AI ever producing anything that could be regarded as art:

> As machine intelligence develops, we imagine that some artists who work with it will draw the same critique levelled at early photographers. An unsubtle critic might accuse them of 'cheating', or claim that the art produced with these technologies is not 'real art'. A subtler (but still anti-technological) critic might dismiss

machine intelligence art wholesale as kitsch. As with art in any medium, some of it undoubtedly *will* be kitsch – we have already seen examples – but some will be beautiful, provocative, frightening, enthralling, unsettling, revelatory, and everything else that good art can be.[28]

If photography, as Walter Benjamin has claimed, challenges the *aura* of a work of art, what does AI challenge?[29] The problem with AI-generated artwork is not, perhaps, the destruction of *aura* so much as the potential infringement of copyright. This is highlighted by the case of the *Edmond de Bellamy* portrait. Who owns the copyright of the code? What is clear is that a CAN cannot be held responsible for the artwork. A CAN is only the medium through which the artwork was produced. On its own, CAN does not produce the artwork. But who exactly was the author?

Copyright law exists to protect the author and ensure that no one else can plagiarise an artwork. The problem, however, is that copyright law has yet to be adjusted to deal with recent developments in the field of AI. Moreover, the law is very complex and varies from country

FIGURE 3.4 Mario Klingemann, *Memories of Passerby 1* (2018). Mario Klingemann trained a neural network on several thousand portraits from seventeenth to the nineteenth century to generate a never ending stream of disquieting portraits on to two screens.

to country. The art practice Obvious operates in France, and under French law computers cannot claim copyright – copyright can only reside with a human being.[30] And yet curiously under British law copyright rests with 'the person by whom the arrangements necessary for the creation of the work are undertaken'.[31] This, at any rate, was the position taken by Pierre Fautrel of Obvious, who defended their actions: 'We are the people who decided to do this, who decided to print on canvas, sign it as a mathematical formula, put it in a gold frame.'[32]

Beyond this, a further question about authorship is raised. Is the author of an AI-generated work of art the artist or the machine that has been programmed? Klingemann is quite clear that the author remains the artist:

> If you heard someone playing the piano, would you ask? 'Is the piano the artist?' No. So, same thing here. Just because it is a complicated mechanism, it doesn't change the roles . . . The typewriter enables someone to write a book. Well, for me, the keyboard enables me to write code, and then, well yes, there are neural networks involved that maybe you could say that they are my brushes that I learn to use.[33]

Indeed the history of art has also been a history of new techniques and new technologies. As much as the invention of perspective changed the way in which art was produced, more recent developments in materials and technologies have equally changed the way in which art has developed.

Referring to his artwork *Memories of Passersby 1*, an AI-generated work that continuously produces portraits of non-existent people, Klingemann observes:

> The machine that I created will keep on generating portraits of non-existing people for ever, and it can do that because it uses a collection of neural networks and in this case I used portraits painted by the great masters from Western European art history. And, yes, so now the machine is in a cycle where it continuously creates new faces that start changing, that fade away. And it observes itself. It creates a feedback loop.[34]

But could we not also ask whether the process of feeding a machine data consisting of the artworks of others is not simply a form of reproduction of these artworks? This, however, begs the question as to what is the original. Would a collage be viewed as a copy or an original? And could we not also ask whether anything is truly original, since culture itself is propagated through memes – through a kind of copying?[35]

In training the machine to produce an artwork, the crucial issue for Klingemann is control. He compares the training of the machine, to the training of children. We can do our best to train them, but in the end they are beyond our control:

It's not a rendered video, or a curated print, or curated images that I preselected. It is doing it at that moment, which is a risky thing, because it's a system where you only have a certain amount of foresight as to what it might do. But, in the end, it's always this feedback between me the artist and the medium and the material. And it is at least like a child where I can say, 'Now, you go out in the world alone, and I can trust you that you can keep on doing what I hoped that you would do, even if I am not sitting next [to you] and still able to change something.' So that is kind of like a hard moment for me to say, 'Now I believe it's okay to take my hands off the keyboard, and let it out in the world.'[36]

And so, is Klingemann responsible for the artwork, or has he delegated all responsibility to the machine? One way to answer this question might be to reflect on how artists have always operated. Indeed, we should perhaps question whether the standard training at any art school is so different. Every artist graduating from an art school has been trained – *schooled* – in an educational system that arguably exerts greater influence than the traditionally liberal-minded art world would wish to admit. How is this so different from the way a neural network is trained? Meanwhile, could we not also argue that this is no different to the ateliers of the past? After all, many leading artists would delegate much of their work to apprentices and expect them to complete it in the style of the master.

This is also not so dissimilar to contemporary architectural practices, where a number of junior architects and interns are employed to produce designs in the manner of that practice. Thus, for example, Zaha Hadid established a certain, highly recognisable aesthetic that has now become the in-house 'style' for Zaha Hadid Architects (ZHA), and those working for ZHA have to work within those aesthetic constraints, even though Hadid herself has passed away. Likewise, we have seen how AI can hallucinate new ZHA-like designs based on a dataset of previous ZHA designs. How would this be any different to Klingemann and his 'children' being unleashed into the world to 'paint' in a manner in which they were 'trained'?

Rethinking creativity

Up until now the dominant tradition has been to judge creativity in terms of the end product. This is based largely on the thinking of Margaret Boden, who has drawn up a series of categories by which to classify creativity. Boden distinguishes between what she calls psychological creativity (P-creativity) and historical creativity (H-creativity).[37] P-creativity could be defined as something novel in terms of the person who created it, whereas H-creativity refers to something that has been created for the first time in history.

Boden further divides creativity into three distinct 'types' or genres of creativity – combinational, exploratory and transformational.[38] Combinational creativity 'produces unfamiliar combinations of familiar ideas, and works by making associations between ideas that were only indirectly linked'.[39] For Boden, collage would be an example of combinational creativity. Exploratory creativity, meanwhile, is based on a culturally accepted style of thinking, or 'conceptual space', defined by a set of generative rules. Painting, architecture and music, and artistic production in general, would be examples of exploratory creativity, and Boden cites a shape grammar study of the works of Frank Lloyd Wright, which suggested many other possible designs that could have been produced.[40] Importantly, for Boden, exploratory creativity can also lead to transformational creativity.[41] Finally, in transformational creativity, 'the space or style is transformed by altering (or dropping) one or more of its defining dimensions'.[42] Science offers some of the best examples of transformational creativity, where paradigmatic shifts in knowledge can occur. This can lead to surprising – or even shocking – results, as something might have been generated that could never have been previously imagined. According to Boden, then, creativity can be categorised according to its 'type' or genre. However, the three categories of creativity that Boden lists – combinational, exploratory and transformational – appear to be more like *creative strategies* than creativity itself. Architect Thom Mayne, for example, deploys what he calls 'combinatorial design' in the architectural design process. This sounds similar to Boden's notion of 'combinational creativity'. But for Mayne this is not a form of creativity as such, but simply a design strategy. Nor does a design strategy guarantee creativity. Boden claims, for example, that collage is an example of combinational creativity, and collage is certainly an artistic strategy, but an artwork generated using collage might not necessarily be so creative.

There appear to be a number of shortcomings, then, in Boden's approach. She seems to categorise creativity in terms of the *outcome*. But should we not understand creativity in terms of the *process* of creation itself? Creativity might well be involved in generating a design, but creativity, surely, is what *feeds* that process. Indeed, for many designers creativity is a question of how the design process unfolds in relation to the affordances of the materials and tools being used.[43] What applies to design clearly also applies to all fields of creativity. As Ben Ceverny comments, 'Sculpture is not in the result. The sculpture is in the process.'[44] It makes little sense, then, to judge creativity in terms of the outcome of that process. This would be akin to judging a building in terms of its 'style'.[45] Indeed Boden uses the term 'style' frequently in her discussion of creativity.[46] An historian or an outside commentator might judge a work in terms of the outcome, but for the designer creativity is expressed, surely, in the very process of design.[47]

Boden's approach, then, tends to reduce creativity to a limited range of outcomes. But should not creativity be understood as a pervasive sensibility that is infused throughout the behaviour of a creative individual, and expressed in various ways? Would creative individuals not express their creativity in every facet of their existence, from the way they dress and behave, through to the actual works that they produce? Besides, we are never likely to fully comprehend the nature of the creative process since, as Arthur Miller has argued, much of it belongs to the realm of the unconscious.[48] Indeed, for Freud, fantasies can be expressed in sublimated form in the creative act.[49] The creative individual might therefore be unaware of what is influencing the creative process.[50]

Moreover, we must at least challenge the notion that creativity can be judged in such an objective fashion. Who is in a position to even *judge* creativity? And what if a creative act is not recognised by that judge?[51] Could we not say that van Gogh was creative, even though his creative abilities were not recognised in his lifetime? And how are we to appraise the creativity of Move 37 in the match between Lee Sedol and AlphaGo, if the creativity of that move is not even recognised until much later? Might we draw a distinction between human creativity and absolute creativity, just as we have drawn a distinction between human intelligence and absolute intelligence? Does creativity, perhaps, lies in the eye of the beholder? Or does creativity exist in the mind of the creative individual? In order to fully understand the creative process, should we not take into account the background sensibilities and aspirations that feed into that process? And does it even make sense to distinguish between P-creativity and H-creativity? What if an individual creates something without knowing whether someone else has created it before? In short, is it not time to revisit the question of creativity?

This is not the place, however, to offer a comprehensive redefinition of creativity. The issue of creativity is a highly complex one – even

FIGURE 3.5 Scott Eaton, *Hyperbolic Composition 1* (2019). Scott Eaton works in collaboration with AI, training a neural network to turn one of his own drawings into a figurative representation.

more complex, as Anil Seth has observed, than the thorny problem of consciousness itself.[52] But even if we are not yet in a position to redefine creativity in any meaningful way, we can at least ask some provocative questions that challenge previously held assumptions about creativity.

In the mirror of AI

Digital simulations can often help us to understand analogue behaviours. For example, it wasn't until Craig Reynolds had produced a digital model for the flocking behaviour of birds, using 'boids', that we were able to understand the behaviour of actual birds.[53] This is not to say that AI would serve as a 'digital model' of human intelligence – since, for the moment at least, AI cannot track the human brain – but nonetheless the principles that govern AI might offer some clues about the principles that govern human intelligence. Could AI, then, provide us with a mirror in which to understand certain aspects of human intelligence, such as learning, consciousness and even creativity itself?

Take a neural network. Although modelled only loosely on the brain, a neural network might help us to understand how the brain actually works. Both are black boxes, in that we know that they work, but do not fully understand *how* they work. But might they share certain similarities? Might the brain, for example, also perform some form of backpropagation, as Geoffrey Hinton speculates?[54] After all, although it had previously been assumed that the synapses in the brain operate in only one direction – feed forward – it has now been argued that they might operate in both directions – both feed forward and feed backwards.[55] And could this principle allow the brain to critique or correct itself, just as backpropagation allows for the neural network to correct errors? Even if the brain does not operate in *exactly* the same way, it seems to be doing something similar. As Joshua Bengio observes, 'Backpropagation works incredibly well, and it suggests that maybe the brain is doing something similar – not exactly the same, but with the same function.'[56]

Or let us take the logic of DeepDream. From an architectural perspective, what makes DeepDream so fascinating is that the technique of 'inverting the network' reverses the flow of a neural network. Instead of interpreting or critiquing an image, a neural network can now generate an image. What implications might this have for architectural culture? Take the distinction between the architectural critic and architectural designer. Typically, the architectural critic tends to be more critical, while the architectural designer tends to be more capable of generating forms. Does the reversal in direction of operation suggest that the process of architectural criticism is – in some senses – the opposite to the process of architectural form generation? Does this phenomenon therefore help to explain why architectural critics tend to be more inhibited when it comes to form generation, while architectural designers tend to be less critical?

And if criticism is understood as the opposite of form generation, does this opposition not play out in the training of a GAN, where the generator/artist and the discriminator/critic train each other? And could we extend this model to the training of the architect, where architectural students are encouraged to be more critical in the generation of their design and more imaginative in their criticism? Could the role of criticism, in other words, echo that of backpropagation in correcting errors and improving a design? Could we therefore say that genuine creativity emerges out of the interaction of form generation and criticism? Might we even speculate, then, that creativity can be understood as an emergent property?

'Could AI become a
mirror in which to
understand human
creativity?'

Hiroshi Ishiguro remarks about robots, 'The robot is a kind of mirror that reflects humanity and by creating intelligent robots we can open up new opportunities to contemplate what it means to be human.'[57] Could we say something similar about AI? Could AI become a mirror in which to understand human creativity?

4

AI, media art and neuroscience

The movie *Blade Runner* (1982), directed by Ridley Scott, depicts a dystopian future world involving 'replicants' – bio-engineered robots – manufactured by the Tyrrell Corporation to have superhuman abilities so they can survive in the hostile conditions of off-world colonies. Replicants are therefore potentially dangerous, and as a safety measure are given a limited lifespan of four years. In the movie a group of six replicants return to earth in a bid to extend their lives. Rick Deckard, played by Harrison Ford, is a 'blade runner', a kind of policeman/bounty hunter, charged with hunting down and 'retiring' – killing – these replicants. The problem, however, is that replicants – especially the advanced Nexus 7 model – look almost identical to human beings and can only be distinguished by using the elaborate 'Voight-Kampff' test designed to check whether their emotional responses and eye reflexes meet the standard of human beings. The movie is thus primarily about the difference between human beings and replicants, such that replicants become a mirror in which to understand what it is to be human. As the late Rutger Hauer, who plays the leader of the replicants, Roy Batty, comments, 'In many ways, Blade Runner wasn't about the replicants. It was about what does it mean to be human.'[1]

Fast-forward to now – not so long after 2019, the year in which Blade Runner was set – and it is worth reflecting on how prescient the movie has proved to be.[2] We do not have replicants infiltrating society, but we do have AI personal assistants, Siri, Alexa and Google Assistant, colonising our everyday lives, and we do have AI filtering our spam, and performing other tasks on our cell phones. We don't have flying cars, but we do have Maglev trains, drones and self-driving cars. We do not have the Tyrrell Corporation, but corporate life is dominated nonetheless by hi-tech companies, such as Google, Amazon, Apple and Microsoft. And, as predicted in *Blade Runner*, we do talk to our computers and do have LED advertising all over our buildings, especially in cities like Shanghai. Clearly, *Blade Runner* has proved to be highly prescient.

Although replicants are not necessarily controlled by AI, they are clearly an artificial life form endowed with some kind of 'intelligence'. There are other parallels too. The victory of Batty over Tyrrell in the game of chess in *Blade Runner* foreshadows the victory of DeepBlue over Kasparov in 1997. Moreover, the role of the 'Voight-Kampff' test in detecting replicants echoes the use of the Turing Test to determine how convincing AI can be, just as in a GAN the discriminator determines how convincing the output of the generator is. They therefore make a productive vehicle by which to address the topic of AI, especially in the context of debates about human intelligence.

Blade Runner is based on the novel by Philip K Dick, *Do Androids Dream of Electric Sheep?* It therefore opens up the provocative question of whether AI can dream. The theme of dreaming, of course, runs throughout *Blade Runner*. With this very title, the author raises an important question about the potential of androids/robots to 'dream'. Indeed the theme of dreaming runs throughout both *Blade Runner* movies. In *Blade Runner*, Deckard has a dream of a unicorn, while in the sequel, *Blade Runner 2049*, Anna Stelline, whom we discover is the daughter of Deckard and his lover, Rachael, is a designer of dreams for replicants.[3] Since replicants are not born and brought up like humans, they need to be given dreams, just as they need to be given memories.

Dreaming machines

The Japanese computational architect and AI expert Makoto Sei Watanabe has been exploring the potential of AI in architecture since 1994.[4] After a series of investigations, however, Watanabe became somewhat frustrated, realising that while human beings have their

PLATE 7 Refik Anadol, *Quantum Memories*, Melbourne, Australia (2020). To generate these extraordinary images, Anadol used a generative algorithm enabled by AI and quantum computing to produce an artwork that reflects the collective memory of nature. Refik Anadol.

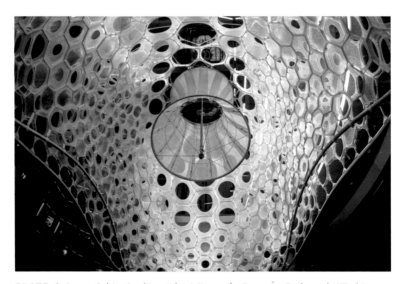

PLATE 8 Jenny Sabin Studio, *Ada*, Microsoft Campus, Redmond, Washington (2019). Ada is a lightweight knitted pavilion structure composed of digitally knit responsive and data-driven tubular and cellular components, that uses AI to detect facial expressions and sounds that are translated into an immersive, interactive experience of colour and light. The name of the project is a reference to Ada Lovelace. *Ada* by Jenny Sabin Studio for Microsoft Research. Artists in Residence program 2018–2019. Image by Jake Knapp courtesy Microsoft Research.

PLATE 5 Refik Anadol, *WDCH Dreams*. In order to make Walt Disney Concert Hall 'dream', Refik Anadol used a creative, computerized 'mind' to mimic how humans dream. Refik Anadol.

PLATE 6 Refik Anadol, *Machine Hallucinations*, Artechouse, New York (2019). Refik Anadol's installation at the Artechouse digital art space in New York consists of a 30-minute-long machine hallucination generated from millions of photos of New York City. Refik Anadol.

PLATE 3 Mario Klingemann, *The Butcher's Son* (2017). This GAN-generated artwork was the first AI-generated artwork to win a major international prize, when it was awarded the Lumen Prize in 2018. *The Butcher's Son*, Mario Klingemann 2017.

PLATE 4 Memo Akten, *Gloomy Sunday* (2017). In this experiment, Akten shows how a neural network trained on images of flowers will read flowers into everything that it sees. Memo Akten.

PLATE 1 Sofia Crespo, *Realisation* (2018). In her *Neural Zoo* series, Sofia Crespo uses neural networks to extract patterns and features from natural systems and represent them in a way that both echoes the natural world and yet also appears patently artificial. Sofia Crespo.

PLATE 2 Sofia Crespo, *Courage* (2018). In her *Neural Zoo* series, Sofia Crespo uses neural networks to extract patterns and features from natural systems and represent them in a way that both echoes the natural world and yet also appears patently artificial. Sofia Crespo.

was lit up by a data sculpture projected on to its exterior. The data sculpture had been generated by Anadol in collaboration with Google AMI and computational sound engineer Parag Mital.[22] This was not the first time that Anadol had projected his work on to buildings. Nor was Anadol the first to explore the use of AI within the realm of architecture. But nonetheless, the symbolic significance of projecting a data sculpture of such magnitude on to such a prominent architectural masterpiece marked a threshold moment in the introduction of AI to the world of architecture. It was also, arguably, the moment when a sense of *Blade Runner* was brought to the architecture of LA. Anadol and his team had not only succeeded in bringing the WDCH alive: 'Architecture is not any more alone, dark in the late night.'[23] As Alejandro Iñárrito commented, 'It was the first time that I could touch "science fiction".'[24]

The projection of the data sculpture on to the WDCH was not the first time that Anadol had projected data sculptures on to buildings. In fact he had begun to attract attention with a series of data-driven works projected on to interiors of buildings. His early work *Infinity*

FIGURE 4.2 Refik Anadol, *Machine Hallucinations*, Artechouse, New York (2019). To create this machine hallucination, Anadol used a customised StyleGAN algorithm to process every single available photographic memory of New York City.

Room (2015) draws upon his childhood dreams and memories, two domains that play a significant role in his work.[25] As such, *Infinity Room* (2015) opens the door not only to memories and dreams, but also to the potential of hallucinating about a space. Likewise his *Virtual Depictions: San Francisco* (2015), a data-based work projected on to a wall in the entrance lobby of a building designed by Skidmore Owens and Merrill (SOM) in San Francisco. This artwork was based on a real-time data sculpture pipeline, combining geo-location-tagged Twitter activities and 3D point cloud data of the city. Other installations, such as *Wind of Boston* (2017), based on weather data, and *Bosphorus* (2018), based on radar data, continued this series of data sculptures displayed on the walls of buildings.[26]

Anadol's *Infinite Space* (2019) project for Artechouse in New York is a further development of AI-based techniques developed for his WDCH project.[27] Here, however, he uses them to simulate the effect of synthetic architectural 'memories' of the city of New York. Anadol and his team downloaded more than 213 million publicly available photographs of buildings in the city. They then introduced an algorithm to remove any photos with people in them, reducing the

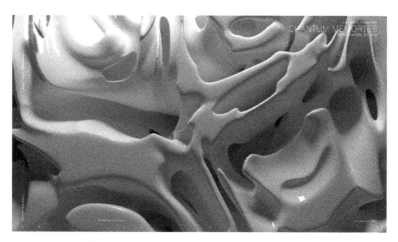

FIGURE 4.3 Refik Anadol, *Quantum Memories*, Melbourne, Australia (2020). To generate this project, Anadol processed more than 200 million nature-related images using quantum computing software, in collaboration with Google AI Quantum.

number to 9.5 million images. And they then introduced another algorithm to allow the machine to 'dream' based on this dataset, and projected the resulting 30-minute movie on to the interior space, a disused boiler room turned into an exhibition space.[28] A further development from this is the Quantum Memories project (2020), exploring the potential of quantum computing.

Anadol is also responsible for generating the image on the front cover of this book, using a customised version of StyleGANs.[29] As is self-evident, the image resembles a design by Zaha Hadid Architects (ZHA). This is hardly surprising, in that it was 'hallucinated' by AI, based on a dataset of images of designs by ZHA. The output is clearly influenced by the input of ZHA images. Importantly, it is not a copy of any one of those images, but an interpolation based on the overall dataset. Furthermore, it is not an image of anything that already exists, but a hallucination of something that could exist.

Machine hallucinations

The term often used to describe AI generated images is 'machine hallucinations'. Although we might think that 'machine hallucinations' are fundamentally different to human hallucinations, there are surprising similarities, and we can make direct comparisons between how AI operates and how we ourselves operate.[30] In fact, AI sees the world through the lens of the data on which it has been trained, just as we also see the world through the lens on which we have been trained. For example, if we were to ask anyone how many colours there are in a rainbow, the chances are that they would reply, 'seven', even though there are an infinite number of colours in the spectrum that constitutes a rainbow.[31] This is because we are trained at school to understand that there are seven colours in a rainbow. And, if we were to ask any architect what a 'functionalist' building looks like, the chances are they would describe a white building on *piloti* with a flat roof, even though flat roofs are not very functional in most countries because they tend to leak. This is because we are trained at architecture school to understand that functionalist buildings have flat roofs.

The idea that we are conditioned to see the world in a certain way comes under the theory of 'predictive perception', a theory that is beginning to gain some traction in neuroscience.[32] According to neuroscientist Anil Seth, the brain is locked into a boney skull without any light or sound, and has little information about the outside world apart from electrical impulses. As such, the brain tries to offer its 'best guess' as to what is happening out there, based on sensory information and previous experiences. Perception is therefore not as objective as it might seem. Nor is it simply a question of the brain receiving signals from the outside. The brain actively partakes in trying to make sense of what it is sensing:

> Instead of perception depending largely on signals coming into the brain from the outside world, it depends as much, if not more, on perceptual predictions flowing in the opposite direction. We don't just passively perceive the world, we actively generate it. The world we experience comes as much, if not more, from the inside out as from the outside in.[33]

Seth argues that the brain therefore makes predictions – or 'hallucinations', as he calls them – about what it is perceiving. But these hallucinations need to be reined in so as to prevent incorrect predictions. There needs to be a degree of control involved. Seth illustrates this with a video processed using a DeepDream algorithm that shows how overly strong perceptual predictions can lead to weird hallucinatory perceptions, where the viewer comes to read images of dogs into everything that they see.[34] This leads Seth to conclude that if hallucination is a form of uncontrolled perception, then perception itself must be a form of 'controlled hallucination':[35]

> If hallucination is a kind of controlled perception, then perception right here and right now is also a kind of hallucination, but a controlled hallucination in which the brain's predictions are being reined in by sensory information from the world. In fact, we're all hallucinating all the time, including right now. It's just that when we agree about our hallucinations, we call that reality.[36]

What is interesting here is that Seth also uses DeepDream to illustrate the way in which we see the world through a form of predictive perception. Moreover, just as we use the expression 'machine hallucinations' to describe the images generated through deep learning, Seth uses the expression 'controlled hallucinations' to describe the process of predictive perception on the part of humans. According to this logic, when we look at the world we are actively hallucinating, similar to how machines are 'hallucinating' when they generate images. There is an implicit parallel being drawn, then, between human perception and computational image generation. The two would appear to be not as dissimilar as we might at first imagine.

Similarly, computational artist Memo Akten uses artificial neural networks to illustrate how we are trained to see the world:[37] In his 'Gloomy Sunday' interactive experiment, Akten offers an illustration of how an artificial neural network interprets objects based on how it has been trained. Thus, if trained on a dataset composed solely of images of flowers, the artificial neural network will read images of flowers into everything that it sees. As Akten observes, 'The picture we see in our conscious mind is not a mirror image of the outside world, but is a reconstruction based on our expectations and prior beliefs.'[38] By extension, previous experiences act as a kind of filter to subsequent experiences. They distort and colour how we see the world. In other words, Akten's notion that perception is based on 'prior beliefs' appears to be remarkably similar to Seth's notion that it is based on 'previous experiences'. Similarly, Akten's 'Gloomy Sunday' experiment, which used trained neural networks, is remarkably close Seth's experiment using DeepDream. In short, Akten appears to be corroborating Seth's theory of predictive perception.

Equally, we could compare Seth's notion of the 'controlled hallucination' at work in our perception of the world with Slavoj Zizek's notion of 'fantasy' that serves as a lens through which we perceive the world. Zizek's view is grounded in Lacanian thinking. According to Lacan, we do not access the 'Real' except in moments of *jouissance*.[39] What we take for the real is not the real in itself, but an appearance of reality.[40] In fact our perception of reality comes to us 'via a detour through the maze of the imagination'. It is coloured and distorted by our imagination, no less than our outlook on the world is distorted by the way that we have been trained to view the world, as the two 'experiments' by Seth and Akten illustrate. Moreover, for Zizek, our perception of reality is a *fantasy* of reality.[41] Fantasy, then, plays a key role in how we understand 'reality'. In fact

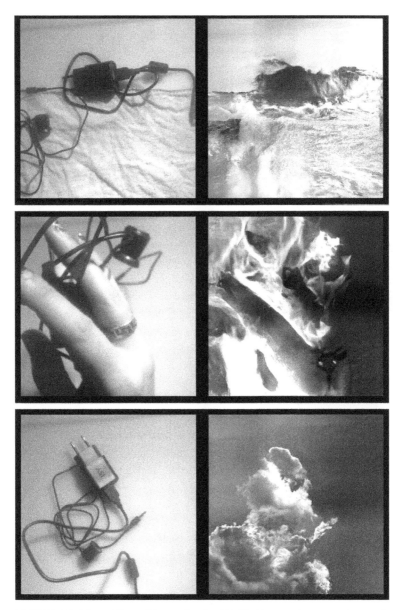

FIGURE 4.4 Memo Akten, *Gloomy Sunday* (2017). Akten trains a neural network with different sets of images: water, fire and clouds. He then uses the neural network, trained in this way, to become a 'lens' through which to look at everyday objects on a table. As a result, the network reads water, fire and clouds into everything that it sees on the table.

fantasy, for Zizek, is literally 'constitutive of how we see reality': 'Far from being a kind of fragment of our dreams that prevents us from "seeing reality as it effectively is", fantasy is constitutive of what we call reality: the most common bodily "reality" is constituted via a detour through the maze of imagination.'[42]

Zizek goes further, and speculates whether, as we use computation to simulate human thought ever more closely, an inversion might take place, such that human thought begins to emulate a computer programme, and our own understanding of the world itself becomes a model:

> What if this 'model' is already a model of the 'original' itself, what if human intelligence itself operates like a computer, is 'programmed', etc.? The computer raises in pure form the question of semblance, a discourse which would not be a simulacrum: it is clear that the computer in some sense only 'simulates' thought; yet how does the total simulation of thought differ from 'real' thought?[43]

In other words, Zizek is speculating that we might be living in a simulation, an argument originally floated by sociologist Jean

FIGURE 4.5 Fernando Salcedo, *Deep Perception* (2020). This is a study using a CycleGAN trained on images of the King Abdullah Petroleum Studies and Research Center, Ryadh, Saudi Arabia to reinterpret images of clothing on the left to produce a hallucination of other possible designs for that building.

Baudrillard and made famous in the movie, *The Matrix*, but since supported by other more recent philosophical arguments.[44] Likewise, we can draw comparisons between this view and the way that Seth and other neuroscientists understand our conception of the world as a constructed one, based on prior beliefs and experiences, such that what we perceive is also a model – a simulation – of the world. This leads Zizek to conclude that it would be wrong to denigrate 'virtual reality' as a lesser form of reality. What virtual reality reveals is not how 'virtual' virtual reality is, but rather how 'virtual' our understanding of 'reality' is: 'The ultimate lesson of virtual reality is the virtualization of the very true reality.'[45]

Architecturalisations

Turning to architecture, could we not also compare the way that we are trained as architects to the way in which artificial neural networks are trained? In 2020, FIU architectural student Fernando Salcedo undertook an interactive AI experiment not dissimilar to 'Gloomy Sunday', where he trained a neural network on two sets of images, one based on generic modernist architecture and the other based on the King Abdullah Petroleum Studies and Research Center designed by ZHA.[46] The neural network then read architectural forms into everything that it sees, including items of clothing, through a process similar to the principle of predictive perception. In this weirdly distorted view of the world, a simple tie can be read as a tower block, and a crumpled shirt can be read as a warped version of the ZHA project. Importantly, however, the neural network is not reading forms in an objective fashion. Rather, it is reading them through a filter.[47] This experiment provokes some interesting questions. Is this perhaps how architects see the world, reading potential buildings into everything that they see?[48] In other words, through their architectural education are architects *trained* to see the world in a certain way, just as a neural network is trained to see the world?

To claim that this is the case would be to mount an argument based on pure analogy. In and of itself, this experiment does not prove anything. Nonetheless it is tempting to pursue this line of enquiry further. For example, might this experiment not offer us insights into the nature of inspiration itself – the 'act' of reading the world through a particular lens and then re-expressing that vision in the design itself?

We could describe this process as a form of 'architecturalisation'. In effect, architects tend to 'architecturalise' whatever they see, and read the world in architectural terms.[49] This allows them to be inspired by any number of non-architectural items – biological entities, animals, insects, geological formations and indeed potentially anything – and incorporate them into their architectural expressions.[50] This might explain, for example, how Jorn Utzon was inspired by the billowing sails of yachts and went on to read them as potential vaults for an opera house overlooking Sydney Harbour. This might also help to explain why architects so often misinterpret philosophical concepts, such as the 'fold' promoted by Gilles Deleuze, and assume they are references to architectural forms, even though they have nothing to do with form, or architecture as such.[51] It might also explain how some architects and architectural commentators make the mistake of taking terms referring to the digital – terms such as 'discrete' or 'pixelation' – and assume that they are referring potentially to architectural forms, even though the digital itself is immaterial and has no form.[52]

By extension, it would also explain why architects tend to 'aestheticise' everything they see, reading the world in terms of aesthetic concerns, and rinsing it of any economic or social and political considerations.[53] Why is it, for example, that many architects have a tendency to privilege design concerns over economic factors, even though economic factors are the driver of any design? Indeed, why are there so few references to economic considerations in books on architecture, apart from the cost of the book on the back cover? It is as though architects always tend to see the world with a certain gaze, as though through rose-tinted, aestheticising lenses.

It is important to understand, then, that the gaze of the architect is not neutral. It has been trained, no less than a neural network has been trained. Whether we understand this conditioned outlook in Seth's terms as a form of 'controlled hallucination' or in Zizek's terms as being constituted through 'fantasy', it is clear that architects see the world not as it is but as they are trained to see it. But is this not so dissimilar to the message behind the term 'deconstruction' coined by Derrida?

Derrida argues that our perception of the world carries with it certain biases, just as the data used in AI carries with it certain biases.[54] Our perception of the world is therefore 'constructed'. And this 'constructed' perception is a distorted one, as we have seen with the standard interpretation of a rainbow. What needs to be exposed, then, is how our understanding of the world has been 'constructed'. And this 'constructed' way of understanding the world itself needs to be 'deconstructed'. The same issue applies to architecture.

'Let us never forget,' writes Derrida, 'that there is an architecture of architecture.'[55] Put another way, our understanding of architecture is itself 'constructed', as we have seen with the standard perception of 'functionalism' as referring to buildings with flat roofs. Our understanding of architecture therefore needs to be 'deconstructed'. The irony here is that architects largely misinterpret Derrida. They tend to think that the term 'deconstruction' refers in some way to the construction of architecture, whereas in fact it is simply an architectural metaphor.[56]

What is this misinterpretation, then, but yet another example of architecturalisation?

Can machines dream?

Is Watanabe correct, then, to argue that machines do not have dreams?[57] Arguably, we could claim that machines can now 'dream'. The term 'dream', after all, appears throughout Anadol's descriptions of his work. It also appears in the name of the technique DeepDream, and the Autodesk software Dreamcatcher. We can also find references to other dream-like ways of generating images, such as 'hallucinations'. Mitchell, of course, argues that AI would require consciousness in order to appreciate the artistic quality of anything that it generates. Consciousness, for Mitchell, is therefore the hallmark of creativity.[58] But do dreams themselves necessarily depend on consciousness?

According to Freud, dreams have many roles. For example, repressed feelings can be expressed in dreams, just as they can erupt involuntarily in speech through the process of *parapraxis*, or can be expressed in sublimated form in any creative act. Equally dreams offer a 'royal road' to the unconscious, as Freud puts it, as they give access to parts of the mind inaccessible during conscious thought.[59] In other words, dreams themselves do *not* necessarily have anything to do with consciousness and can be present in sublimated form in the creative act of designing. Seen from this perspective, dreams do not depend on consciousness.

Alternatively, we could argue that in terms of the discourse of 'extended intelligence', the generation of AI work does indeed involve consciousness. It is just that the human being, and not AI, possesses consciousness. In fact we could even argue that this is always the case in any computational operation, in that the computer is never acting on its own. Ultimately the user remains in charge.[60] Despite the seemingly objective nature of the computational process, the output must always satisfy the subjective user. And if the output does not satisfy the user, then the algorithms can always be tweaked until they produce a result that *does* satisfy the user.

As such, it is almost meaningless to talk about AI in isolation. For the moment at least, it is always a question of a form of human–AI collaboration: less artificial intelligence per se, more 'extended intelligence'. And, since the user has consciousness, by definition this collaboration itself involves consciousness. Seen in this light, it is simply a matter of the user dreaming *through* AI, or of the user adopting AI as an extension of the human imagination. Moreover, as many have pointed out, there is only one entity superior to AI, and that is 'humans plus AI'. And clearly 'humans plus AI' are superior to humans without AI. Watanabe's question, then, should not be 'Can machines dream?' so much as, 'Can humans use machines to enhance their own dreams?'

If we put Watanabe's comments in their full context, however, it is clear that this is actually what Watanabe means. For Watanabe, the secret is not to read AI in isolation, but in terms of a potential AI–human symbiosis. Watanabe refers to AI in this context as a 'capability expanding AI' or an AI that 'can expand the imagination'.

For Watanabe, the working of the brain – in other words, 'intuition' – is always a 'black box'.[61] We cannot understand how it works. Meanwhile AI can also be a 'black box'. In the case of deep learning, for example, even computer scientists don't know quite *how* it works. This symbiosis between machines and humans, then, amounts to a form of 'collaboration' between two black boxes.

Interestingly, Watanabe sees the potential of machines having dreams in terms not of a competition between humans and machines, but of a synthesis, where humans and machines complement each other:

> Will this answer always be true? Will the day come when machines have dreams? Preparing for that day will involve exploring the path of potential cooperation between the brain and machines. This will require work in both areas – white boxes, in other words, the scientific approach or algorithmic design, and black boxes, towards collaborative methodologies, or, in other words, AI Tect. This is similar to how our left and right brains handle different functions and collaborate in delivering an outstanding performance.[62]

And so, do robots dream? And does it even make sense to think of robots in isolation? Or should we only be thinking of robots in collaboration with human beings? Watanabe, at any rate, is interested in this collaboration. Working with robots can help architects to dream up a far greater range of options than their own imagination might allow. Traditionally, we have seen robots as being mechanical devices that can only perform mechanical tasks. But working together with human beings, they can open up space for the imagination. For Michael Hansmeyer this is the crucial step: 'We've been using computers to increase our efficiency and precision. Let us view the computer as our muse, as a partner in design, and as a tool to expand our imagination.'[63]

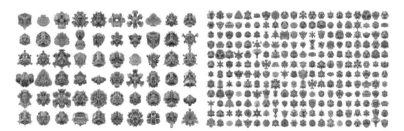

FIGURE 4.6 Michael Hansmeyer, *Learning Beauty in Architecture* (composite image). This research exercise is an investigation into how to measure beauty using a learning machine.

In 2019 there was an exhibition on AI held at the Barbican in London, titled *AI: More than Human*.[64] The premise behind the exhibition was that the concept of AI has to be seen within a broader context as a continuation of a desire to artificially create intelligent life. The exhibition was certainly convincing in making this argument.

The title of the exhibition, however, appears to imply that AI could somehow be 'more than human'. But is it a question of comparison? Should we see the relationship between AI and humans as being one of competition? Is this title not fear mongering? Or should we see the

'Is the role of AI to allow us to become more human?'

role of AI as being complementary to the role of humans? Isn't one of the roles of AI to free us from the drudgery of certain repetitive operations and allow us to expand our own all too human imagination? Is the role of AI to allow us to become more human?

AI, be my muse!

5

AI and architecture

The exhibition *The Architectural Beast*, curated by Hernán Díaz Alonso and designed by Casey Rehm, opened in the FRAC Centre, Orléans, France on 11 October 2019. This was the first exhibition using AI at a major architectural gallery.[1] The exhibition comprised the work of seventeen architects and artists from the

FIGURE 5.1 *The Architectural Beast* (2019), Fonds Régional d'Art Contemporain (FRAC) Biennale in Orléans, France. *The Architectural Beast* was an exhibition curated by Hernan Diaz Alonso. The AI aspects of the exhibition were designed by Casey Rehm, with the support of Laure Michelon, Jiahao Ye, Damjan Jovanovic and Kellan Cartledge.

Deconstructivist Architecture, held at the Museum of Modern Art in New York in 1988, and has remained at the forefront of radical experimentation in architecture.[12] We should also bear in mind that Prix has always been in favour of openness and freedom of expression. Indeed Karl Popper, author of *The Open Society, and its Enemies*, is one of his heroes.[13] Whatever promotes openness is to be celebrated, and whatever closes down opportunities is to be challenged. For Prix, then, we should always be open to the possibilities afforded by AI: 'Don't exclude it! You should integrate it and use it.'[14]

Prix tries to impress on his team how important AI is: 'AI is just a tool. But the most important co-worker in our office is AI.'[15] For Prix, the real benefit of AI is that it can make the design process more efficient and leave more time to explore new languages. For Prix, this comes at a time when architecture is in crisis. Architecture is on 'shaky ground' right now: 'There is almost no gravity.'[16] Architecture is very insecure. The old structures are dying, and 'new structures' are coming up. Although these 'new structures' are not yet ready, there is a possibility that AI might play a role in influencing their development. For Prix, students of architecture need to explore its potential. But AI is not useful if it limits a student's thinking – AI should support their thinking. Without any content, there will be no shape.

At the same time, Prix remains somewhat cautious about AI: 'Is it just a fashion? Will it kill us?'[17] And certainly AI has its limitations. In fact, Prix likes to cite the neuroscientist, Singer, who observes that AI

'Architects should be in the front seat and AI in the back.'

is linear, whereas the human brain is multidimensional. And Prix also warns us against being controlled by an algorithm: 'Be suspicious! Be critical!'[18] Architects should remain in control: 'The architects should be in the front seat, and AI in the back.'[19] Above all, Prix warns us against the zeros and ones of computation leading to a 'zero-zero

FIGURE 5.4 Coop Himmelb(l)au, *DeepHimmelb(l)au* (2020). *DeepHimmelb(l)au* learns to disentangle semantic features that allow specific features to be managed at different levels, thereby generating new interpretations and new worlds. The network allows designers to explore new ways of composition, outside the habitual interpretations. The network is capable of shifting perception on certain features considered meaningful by the designer.

architecture'. And the ultimate analogy for Prix? Not surprisingly, perhaps, for an architect from Vienna, Prix recognises the risk that AI might lead to a kind of ersatz architecture, just like decaffeinated coffee: 'It looks like coffee. It smells like coffee. But no coffee.'[20] But Prix is also amazed by the potential of AI. The most significant foray into AI undertaken so far by Coop Himmelb(l)au is the project *DeepHimmelb(l)au*, an attempt to use CycleGANs and other forms of GANs to 'hallucinate' potential buildings.[21] As mentioned earlier, CycleGANs work with two unpaired datasets. In this case, dataset A is based on reference images of geomorphic formations, and dataset B is based on actual Coop Himmelb(l)au projects. The outcome is a video of a journey through an imaginary landscape of Coop Himmelb(l) au-like building forms. The important point to be stressed here is that these buildings do not actually exist. They are merely 'machine hallucinations'.

DeepHimmelb(l)au has shown us that it is quite possible to 'hallucinate' relatively convincing designs using GANs. Moreover, while there is considerable work that needs to go into preparing the datasets, and many epochs are required to generate a high-quality final product, eventually GANs are capable of generating designs very rapidly. Daniel Bolojan, the computational architect responsible for generating *DeepHimmelb(l)au*[22] has noted, 'As young as it is, within a clearly defined domain, DeepHimmelb(l)au outperforms designers with regards to the speed of interpretation and representation, and the amount of coherent interpretations that it can generate.'[23]

The intention behind *DeepHimmelb(l)au* is to find a way of 'augmenting' design processes, and of adding a layer to already existing designs. The project should also be understood as part of a larger vision for augmenting the design processes in the office. As Bolojan points out, 'Those design processes span from physical models interpretations to real time analysis, real time render, domain translations 2D and 3D, design space explorations.'[24]

DeepHimmelb(l)au, however, also exposes a couple of challenges that need to be addressed before GANs can play a really significant role in an architectural office. Although the images generated by *DeepHimmelb(l)au* appear to be in perspective, they remain 2D images extracted from a video. In order to develop a more convincing and holistic approach, the office would need to move into 3D, and that entails developing more data and using rendering so as to differentiate depth, materiality, layers and so on.[25] One of the most significant challenges of working with most GANs at the moment is shifting from 2D to 3D. Another significant challenge is to develop a technique of controlling images sufficiently, for them to be worked up into architectural drawings.

Morphosis

Pritzker Prize winner and director of Morphosis, Thom Mayne, is also fascinated by the possibilities of AI, although his office has made less progress in the exploration of its potential. Indeed, Mayne has always embraced technological innovation because of the opportunities that it affords. But, for Mayne, no tool – not even AI – is a miracle tool, and human thinking still remains essential. And certainly Mayne sees himself as an analogue person, grounded in the material world, who depends upon others in the office to do the computational work. But computation is important for Mayne, because it promotes a broader approach to thinking. And it has already opened up the office to more flexible approaches to design: 'Digital design allowed us to expand rapidly and allowed us to make some really interesting things to push architecture in terms of potentiality. It opened us up and broke us away from very simplistic, Cartesian fixed systems into dynamic ones.'[26] This is precisely why Mayne is now so enthusiastic about pursuing the potential contributions of AI in his office.

According to Mayne, if we just leave everything to human intuition, we soon run out of ideas. Take Fumihiko Maki, for example, someone who Mayne admires greatly and who taught him as a student in Harvard GSD. However, Maki has not designed anything in twenty years, because he has been unable to reinvent himself – like Le Corbusier – and remain fresh. This is where strategic thinking plays such an important role.

Like Bernard Tschumi, Peter Eisenman and others in his generation, Mayne is interested not so much in the object, but in the relationship between objects, and in developing a strategic approach to design. In particular, Mayne is interested in any approach that challenges *a priori* thinking: '*A priori* thinking is only based on what you know and have seen.'[27] Instead of *a priori* thinking, we should focus on operational strategies, so as to generate output that could never be predicted: 'What became interesting is that you are producing something that is not known. That was infectious. Once you started designing that way, I was only interested in something that I couldn't conceive.'[28]

Mayne has always been impressed by the way that computation can speed up the design process in an architectural office: 'Technology came along, and it replaced that incredibly tedious, in a mechanical sense, process of drawing . . . What technology did was to give us a tool that does that in nanoseconds from incredibly complicated designs that – prior to the adoption of digital technology – had required immensely skilled drafts-people.'[29] Computation, for Mayne, has always been a question of being open to new ideas, and new iterations of existing ideas. 'You're looking for new contemporary processes that rejuvenate you, that give you new material to invent stuff.'[30]

Mayne is also interested in contingency and 'combinatorial design', and the contribution of even a relatively straightforward tool, like Grasshopper (which can be understood as a form of AI in the very broadest sense), so that his office is able to generate a multiplicity of

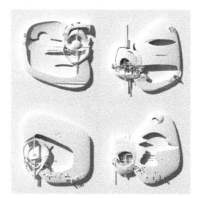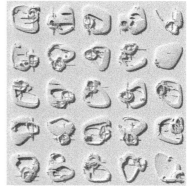

FIGURE 5.5 Morphosis, *Combinatorial Design Studies.* A Grasshopper definition of one formal study is adjusted to provide a range of further combinatorial options.

different options in very little time. When I visited his office, Mayne pointed out some of his iconic formal studies on display, virtuoso works of astonishing sensitivity. What astounds Mayne, however, is that an architect in his office, Daniel Pruske, was able to write a Grasshopper definition for one of them, and then very quickly generate 100 different versions of the same study, by tweaking the constraints and producing iteration after iteration. Mayne again notes, 'I'm looking at these, and I'm saying, "Damn, this is interesting!" This is something that we've got to pursue. Now we are talking about differentiation . . .'[31] Mayne has always been against idealism from a theoretical perspective, but now the computer is allowing him to challenge that notion from a very practical design perspective:

It is interesting to look at this, because it opens up my brain. It doesn't matter if I like it or don't like it. And the idea of 'liking it' or 'not liking it' is kind of thrown away. I've taught *theoretically* about being against the idea of idealism. There's no such thing as an ideal. There's no utopia. There are only options within a contingent world. I now look at this, and say, 'Those are only words.' And now I absolutely cannot tell you there's a favourite scheme. They're different, and they have different qualities. And I'm in a Sophie's choice. I'm looking at two characters. Do I love one more than the other? No, I love them differently. Or I'm looking at faces, and it's not a classically beautiful face. But it's a compelling face, and it's actually more interesting than the classically beautiful one, meaning that you are challenging the notion of beauty.[32]

It is precisely this strategy of combinatorial design – of avoiding any singularity, of opening up beyond the boundaries of intuition, and of cycling through different iterations – that has encouraged Mayne to explore the use of AI in his office.[33] While Grasshopper can generate multiple outcomes, these have to be produced manually one by one over a period of time, whereas the beauty of more advanced AI tools is that they can generate an almost infinite number of options instantaneously. But the challenge for Morphosis is not only how to generate these forms in 3D – the problem that Coop Himmelb(l)au is also facing – but how to control them sufficiently to make them useful within an architectural framework.

Traditional design is inherently intuitive, and therefore subjective.[34] As Watanabe observes, 'Architects are normally not conscious of the mental processes they use to arrive at judgments and selections.'[35] As such, the opportunity afforded by working computationally is to make the design process more objective, by externalising it.[36] The promise of AI techniques is therefore to make design more scientific: 'They make the act of designing – which up to now has been done through experience and intuition – a scientific act.'[37]

The problem with GANs, however, is that there is no way to tell how or why they are performing certain operations. In this sense they are little different to intuition. Both GANs and human intuition are black boxes, as observed earlier. From this perspective, it seems pointless to look for any scientific objectivity in the use of GANs. Satoru Sugihara, a computational architect who has himself worked for Morphosis, summarises the issue:

> While the results of these systems may make sense to us, if we precisely traced the signaling process of neurons and connections one by one, we wouldn't necessarily understand the systems' behavior throughout the entire process. This lack of understanding could be compared to our many hypotheses about human intelligence, in that we still don't understand how our brain activities determine our behavior, even though we can now trace the precise activities of brain neurons.[38]

GANs might be more suited for experimental design, an approach that is searching for novel, surprising and inspirational results that jolt the imagination and open up new possibilities. This in itself is no small contribution. However, the challenge for architects working within professional practice is to design a building operating within a precise controlled set of constraints. After all, architecture is nothing without constraints.

Zaha Hadid Architects

Patrik Schumacher, principal of Zaha Hadid Architects (ZHA), has also been exploring the potential of AI in both the ZHA office and the

AA Design Research Laboratory (DRL). Schumacher's interest in AI, however, is motivated by different concerns. Unlike Prix and Mayne, Schumacher is not interested in speeding up the design process or generating a multiplicity of design options. Rather, he is interested in simulating how spatial organisation might influence social behaviour and – vice versa – how social behaviour might influence spatial organisation, by using populations of AI informed 'agents' to model the behaviour of occupants in Utility AI:

> In both arenas – and they actually feed into each other – ZHA and AA DRL, the use of AI is involved in the development of advanced simulations of occupancy and life processes in built environments and designs we create. We believe that on the level of complexity and dynamism of contemporary social institutions particularly in the world of corporate headquarters and campuses and maybe universities and research campuses . . . that this can no longer be handled with a fixed schedule of accommodation but must involve a more complex sense of what an architectural brief is, namely parametrically variable event scenarios. So these will be simulated with agent populations.[39]

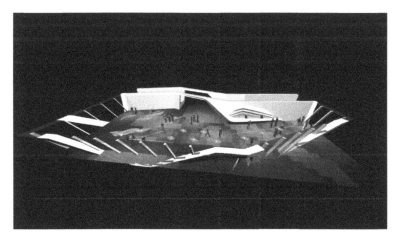

FIGURE 5.6 Daniel Bolojan, *Parametric Semiology Study* (2017). In doctoral research undertaken under Patrik Schumacher, Daniel Bolojan uses ML Algorithms, Decision Trees, and Influence Maps (Gaming AI), implemented in Unity3D, to model the behaviour of human agents in order to test out the layout of a proposed space.

Schumacher refers to his research in this area as 'agent-based parametric semiology'. He uses the term 'semiology' because these environments are 'information rich': 'They are not just physical barriers, and channels and opportunities, but they are full of semantically encoded social protocols, and the societal and situational meanings are embedded and inscribed in these built environments.'[40] The agents therefore need to have the capacity to respond differentially to these semiological codes: 'For instance, for a corporate domain we look at various departmental affiliations, team associations, whether they are outside consultants or internal staff, hierarchy level(s). So they are highly differentiated agents.'[41]

Why does Schumacher use AI for this? Technically, it is quite possible to analyse video footage of actual people in real spaces in order to try to identify the various types of social interaction and the factors that drive that interaction. However, there are limitations to this approach. Not only would it raise privacy issues for those being observed, but it would also be difficult to reconfigure the furniture in order to test out alternative spatial configurations. As a result, computational models are much more suitable, as they can be used to simulate various social scenarios and spatial organisations. This allows data to be collected regarding the type, location and duration of interactions, the characteristics and spatial configuration of the location and so on. And this in turn provides information about the types of social interaction either afforded or prevented by a particular spatial organisation. Finally, machine learning can then be used again to test the intensity of social activity based on a revised spatial organisation.[42] This is another example of how simulations can provide a huge amount of data for subsequent research.[43] It also highlights the potential of using a 'digital twin' to test out the performance of an existing building.[44]

Here, then, we have three contemporary architects with different motivations, each exploring different approaches to the use of AI in their design practices. While Prix is interested in speeding up the design process, Mayne is interested in the potential of differentiation, and Schumacher is interested in testing out the relationship between spatial organisation and social behaviour.[45] This highlights how AI should be understood not as a singular, monolithic technique, but rather as a range of techniques that can be deployed in a variety of different ways.[46]

FIGURE 5.7 AI Build, Daedalus Pavilion, Amsterdam (2016). AI Build made use of Nvidia GPUs for running a combination of computer vision and deep learning algorithms to increase the speed and accuracy in 3D printing a pavilion for a GPU conference in Amsterdam.

AI fabrication

Deep learning is very effective in tasks involving perception. But its capacity to operate in other domains remains relatively limited, as Stuart Russell points out:

> While perception is very important, and deep learning lends itself well to perception, there are many types of ability that we need to give an AI system. This is particularly true when we're talking about activities that take place over a long time span. Or very complex actions like building a factory. There's no possibilities that those kinds of activities can be orchestrated by purely deep learning black-box systems.[47]

To illustrate his point, Russell describes the challenges of trying to use deep learning to build a factory, an example that is highly relevant for architects:

Let's imagine that we try to use deep learning to build a factory. (After all, we humans know how to build a factory, don't we?) So we'll take billions of previous examples of building factories to train a deep learning algorithm; we'll show it all the ways that people have built factories. We take all that data and we put it into a deep learning system and then it knows how to build factories. Could we do that? No, it's just a complete pipe dream. There is no such data, and it wouldn't make any sense, even if we had it, to build factories that way. We need knowledge to build factories. We need to be able to construct plans. We need to be able to reason about physical obstructions, and the structural properties of the building. We can build AI systems to work out these real world systems, but it doesn't achieve it through deep learning. Building a factory requires a different type of AI altogether.[48]

In fact, in and of itself, AI is unable to fabricate anything. The reason for this is straightforward enough. Materials are analogue – and, by extension, so too are buildings – whereas the digital is immaterial. From this perspective, there is no such thing as a digital building.[49] And even when we refer to 'digital fabrication', the actual fabrication relies on analogue processes that have been around since the beginning of time.[50] For what is 3D printing but a form of additive manufacturing, no less than brick laying? And what is Computer Numerically Controlled [CNC] milling, but a form of subtractive manufacturing, no less than carving, chiselling and sawing?[51] As such, the term 'digital fabrication' is misleading. Strictly speaking, we ought to be using the expression, 'digitally *controlled* fabrication', as the term Computer Numerically *Controlled* (CNC) makes clear.[52]

By extension, there is no such thing as 'AI fabrication', although there can be 'AI *controlled* fabrication'. AI consists of algorithms, and algorithms are simply instructions. Algorithms do not fabricate anything. All they can do is to control the fabrication process.[53]

But the issue of 'control' goes further. It can also apply to the questions about perception and motor skills in unstructured environments. Although AI-controlled robots are good at most repetitive tasks, they struggle to deal with relatively simple physical tasks, such as selecting a brick and placing it on top of another. Although this is a relatively simple task for a human, it is quite a challenging one for a

FIGURE 5.8 Alisa Andrasek and Bruno Juričić, *Cloud Pergola*, Croatian Pavilion, Venice Biennale (2018). This structure consists of voxels oriented along a field of vectors and designed with the use of a multi-agent system. The structure was 3D printed with the help of AI Build.

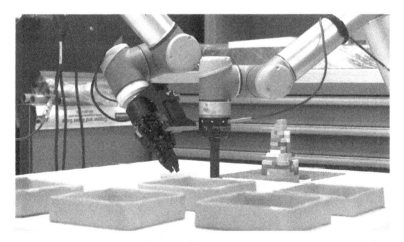

FIGURE 5.9 Autodesk, *Brickbot*. *Brickbot* is a research project from the Autodesk AI Lab that uses computer vision and machine learning to enable a robot to infer what is going on in its environment, then adapt on the fly to accomplish an assigned task. The robot can manipulate toy bricks now, but will soon move on to real-world applications.

robot. As yet – somewhat surprisingly perhaps – robots simply do not have a high enough level of dexterity. As Rodney Brooks wryly observes, 'Everyone's saying robots are coming to take over the world, yet we can't even answer the question of when one will bring us a beer.'[54]

And yet this is precisely the challenge that Autodesk is now addressing. Its new AI research team has been looking at how a robotic arm might learn how to build. The initial challenge was how to get the robotic arm to recognise and pick up Lego bricks and eventually stack them up to form a structure. The answer here is to train the robotic arm not in the physical world, but in a simulated environment by developing a 'digital twin'. Just as AlphaGo ZERO was able to teach itself to play Go through reinforcement learning, by playing games against itself at the extraordinary rate of 20 games per second, so too the Autodesk AI research team has trained the robotic arm in a digital simulation, after many millions of iterations.[55] This opens up a range of possibilities from a robotic arm sorting and stacking bricks completely on its own to an entire assembly line being reconfigured literally overnight.

The ultimate challenge, however, would clearly be to get a robotic arm to stack actual bricks on a construction site. How long will it be before we are able to ask a robot to fabricate something?

Kuka, build me a wall.

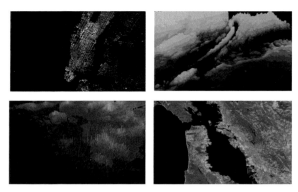

PLATE 9 Shan He, composite image, clockwise from top left: 1. Map of NYC taxi cab pick-ups and drop-offs from 2015, showing pick-up locations in purple and drop-off locations in blue. The size of the circle is based on the distance of the trip. Visualized in Unfolded Studio. Data by nyc.org. 2. Map of NYC elevation made using GeoTIFF raster data from SRTM DEM, hexified by unfolded's data pipeline to 130m diameter H3 hexagons with Kring smoothing. Visualized using Unfolded Studio. 3. NASA's Landsat-8 satellite imagery thermal infrared band of Winter 2020. Visualized in Unfolded studio. 4. Map of building footprints in San Francisco, USA, made in Unfolded studio, coloured by the ground elevation. Data by DataSF. Shan He..

PLATE 10 Theodore, *InFraRed Computer Fluid Dynamics Study*, Vienna, Austria (2020). Creating the dataset is 99 per cent of the work in most real-world applications of Deep Learning models. Apart from highly complex physical simulations, a diverse collection of design inputs is required in order to allow the models to generalize across the vast array of designs found in the real world. City Intelligence Lab, Austrian Institute of Technology, GmbH.

PLATE 11 Biayna Bogosian, *Remote Sensing Study* (2019). Surface-based Remote Sensing of Los Angeles County by Combining Shuttle Radar Topography Mission (SRTM) data with Landsat 8 satellite images. Biayna Bogosian, Surface-based Remote Sensing of Los Angeles County by Combining Shuttle Radar Topography Mission (SRTM) data with Landsat 8 satellite images, 2019.

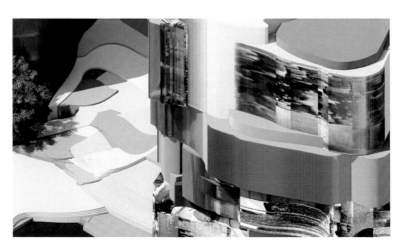

PLATE 12 SPAN, *Peaches and Plums*, High School, Shenzhen, China (2022). This project for a school in Shenzhen, China, was generated using AttnGAN as a driving force in the design process. SPAN Baukunst LLC (Matias del Campo, Sandra Manninger) © 2020.

PLATE 13 Coop Himmelb(l)au, *DeepHimmelb(l)au* (2020). *DeepHimmelb(l)au* is an experimental research project which explores the potential of teaching machines to interpret, perceive, be creative, propose new designs of buildings, augment design workflows and augment architect's/designer's creativity. Coop Himmelb(l)au.

PLATE 14 Casey Rehm, Laure Michelon (Ushida Rehm Studio), Damjan Jovanovic and Lidja Kljakovic (Lifeforms.io), *New Campo Martio Project*, Ars Electronica (2020). *New Campo Marzio* is an open-ended, zero player simulation game powered by AI, based on Giovanni Battista Piranesi's *Campo Marzio* drawing (1762). The simulation utilizes a neural network to learn the features of the original drawing and generate infinite variations of 3D worlds, populated by autonomous agents. lifeforms.io (Damjan Jovanovic and Lidija Kljakovic), 2020.

PLATE 15 Damjan Jovanovic and Lidja Kljakovic (Lifeforms.io), *Dream Estate* (2020). Dream Estate is a self-driven simulation of the world populated by procedurally generated, AI-controlled androids. The simulation relates to the memories of playing with toys and imagining their actions. The toys are seeking interaction and observing new territories. Ushida Rehm Studio/lifeforms.io (Damjan Jovanovic and Lidija Kljakovic), 2020.

6

The future of the architectural office

What role will AI play in the future of the architectural office? From the perspective of the standard architectural office, the most common application of AI is likely to be through AI based software developed by existing architectural software companies, such as Autodesk. In fact much of Autodesk's software, including Fusion 360, is already AI-enabled. The vision at Autodesk – like everywhere else – is not 'AI versus humans' so much as 'AI assisting humans'. AI will take the form of AI assistants – at least for the foreseeable future.

Mike Haley, Senior Director of the Machine Intelligence AI Lab at Autodesk Research, offers his personal prediction of what it will be like to work in the office of the future. According to Haley, we will literally be talking to our computers, and giving instructions based on what we can see on the screen:[1]

Haley 'OK, Autodesk, I want to design a chair.'

Autodesk 'Here are some popular chairs. Scroll through them and select some examples to give me an idea of the type of chair you would like.'

Haley 'OK, I'm making some selections now. Can you show me those together?'

Autodesk 'Alright, here are the chairs you selected.'

Haley 'OK. Those chairs are interesting. Could you combine all possible pairs between those chairs. Find out what's in between them.'

Importantly, the platform allows users to *explore* different options. Hence the name of Spacemaker's recently released generative platform, Explore. Kara Vatn describes how their platform Explore operates: 'With *Explore*, architects and urban planners can continuously generate and review different site proposals, and focus in and iterate at both a macro and micro level. Users can make changes at any point in the planning process and immediately see the impact and alternative options for their site, all in one fast and uninterrupted workflow.'[14]

Not only does their platform serve to increase the range of options, but it also suggests options, some of which might not be immediately apparent. In fact on occasion the platform can come up with suggestions that no architect would ever have imagined, but that nonetheless offer the best solution. Haukeland cites a particular example of a project, affectionately known as their 'Giraffe' project, where the computer was able to find the complete opposite of what an experienced architectural mind might have thought appropriate:

The places where the architects thought that it would be smart to build tall buildings, and the places where they thought it would be smart to build a dense wall, all the things that they intuitively thought would be smart – because they had hundreds of projects of experience – were flipped around. Because when you get the complexity of thinking of a multi-objective organizational problem . . . you are really not able to see the patterns that a computer can find. So what happened was that the computer was able to find a pattern as to how to solve that site that you would never come up with yourself.[15]

Again, the possibility had always existed, but – like move 37 in the AlphaGo match – no one had thought about it before. What this suggests is that from a strategic point of view, planning and the game of Go might have more in common than at first seems apparent.

The platform serves an AI-based assistant, intended not to displace the architect but to serve as a prosthetic extension of the designers' abilities, as Klara Vatn elaborates: '*Explore* isn't replacing creativity. Instead, it provides inspiration. It uses AI to deliver a vast number of options but it is up to the user, using their experience, to select those

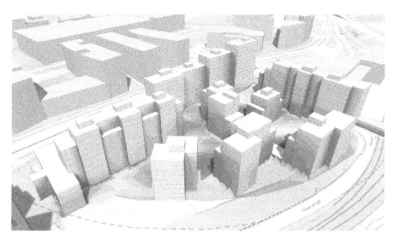

FIGURE 6.3 NREP, Proposal for Okernvelen, Norway, 2020. Spacemaker AI was used to develop seemingly counterintuitive proposals in terms of the handling of sun, view and noise conditions.

that they wish to investigate further; the user is in control, with Spacemaker supporting their decision-making.'[16]

Carl Christensen describes their approach as being similar to how a self-driving car works. A self-driving car relies on AI, but it also relies on many other technologies. Spacemaker is experimenting with a number of different technologies, including deep learning, with a view to incorporating more advanced AI. Although the Spacemaker team does not disclose full details of what they use, for the moment it would seem that their primary focus is on topological optimisation and machine learning, rather than deep learning:

It's a real mix-up of different things, because the core idea is to bring everything together in one platform. So we do use a lot of machine learning, but we do use other algorithms and ways of modelling the world as well. And we generally say that it is AI like a self-driving car is an AI. It's a lot of different things coming together to create a result. So we do use generative design. We use optimization. We use simulation models of the world. We use machine learning models for many things, like surrogate models for understanding the physical environment – for example, how you would change a design to make it better for many factors at once.[17]

Indeed, Christensen sees the role of AI as resting 'on the shoulders of humans' both to guide them and also to give them superpowers, so that humans remain firmly in control: 'To make AI successful, it needs to be on the shoulders of humans, giving them superpowers, and not telling them what to do. That would be like a self-driving car driving where it wants to go.'[18] Nonetheless, as Maria Dantz explains, 'We are an AI platform, but we do want to empower our users. So we

'Architects who use AI will replace those who don't.'

do not believe that AI is going to replace anything. But we do firmly believe that in the workplace of the future architects using AI will replace architects that don't.'[19] This is one of the core beliefs at Spacemaker, and one of potentially huge significance. It is worth repeating: 'In the workplace of the future architects using AI will replace architects that don't.'[20]

One factor that might cause this to happen is a rise in insurance premiums. Just as insurance premiums for human drivers will likely rise in the age of the self-driving car, as human driving skills diminish – making human driving prohibitively expensive – we could imagine that the same might happen with architectural design. AI is able to provide a necessary check not only in terms of risk management but also in terms of error minimalisation, making it an invaluable tool from an insurance perspective. Might we not therefore find that professional indemnity insurance for architects not using AI will skyrocket, forcing architects to use AI, and making good on Spacemaker's prediction that architects using AI will replace those not using AI?

Cedric Price once famously asked, 'Technology is the answer, but what was the question?'[21] By contrast, for Haukeland, 'Technology is just a lever to solve a customer problem.'[22] Haukeland sees their platform as a 'performance driven tool for the masses'.[23] This raises two important issues. On the one hand, it illustrates how AI can be seen not only as an aesthetically-driven design tool, generating some visually striking designs, as we have seen in the previous chapter, but also as a performance-driven design tool, generating cost efficient and performance-based solutions. On the other hand, it highlights how easy it is for everyone to use in an architectural office.

The problem with parametric tools has been that they are often too advanced for many architects to use: 'It was only the parametric geeks in the office that were able to use them.'[24] With AI, however, computation becomes so much easier to use. It is not simply about intelligent trade-offs. It is also a question of recognising the importance of the whole package in offering smart sketching tools and the integration of the whole design process into one consolidated platform. As Haukeland observes:

> I think that you can never make AI the new way of working without really understanding all of the customer needs, and all of the problems, and once you understand that complexity, and what really drives the value, then AI is just empowering that . . . And that's also why I personally really like Carl's analogy of the car, because it's really just about making it easier to drive.[25]

The aim is to provide everyone with tools that are extremely easy to use, and accessible to anyone, no matter how little background experience they have in computation. From this perspective, the Spacemaker model is closer to Haley's model of 'Autodesk, design me a chair' than to Deutsch's model of the superuser.

XKool Technology

Xkool Technology (Xkool) was founded in 2016 by two architects, Wanyu He and Xiaodi Yang. Xkool is a contraction of 'ex-Koolhaas' and refers both to He's previous experience of working under Rem Koolhaas for OMA in Rotterdam and Hong Kong, and to the popular term 'Xkool', which, according to the *Urban Dictionary*, refers to the highest level of

FIGURE 6.4 Xkool (horizontal composite image), StyleGAN-generated building images (2019).

'coolness' that can be achieved.[26] Xkool claims to be 'the world's first innovative technology company that uses cutting-edge technologies such as deep learning, machine learning and big data to successfully apply artificial intelligence to urban planning and architectural design, is based on its own core algorithm technology and in architectural design'.[27] Xkool has also been highly successful in attracting investment. By early 2020, Xkool had secured a joint investment of 100 million RMB from a private equity firm, Vision Night Capital, and a state-owned capital investment firm.[28] Xkool is a 100-plus-person start-up, based in the Vanke Design Commune in Shenzhen, known as the 'Silicon Valley of China', but has further branches in Beijing, Shanghai and Chongqing.

Xkool has developed a cloud-based platform for using AI across a range of scales from interior design to urban planning that can even be accessed from a mobile phone. Like Spacemaker, Xkool also caters for the property development market, although 70 per cent of its users are architects. And like Spacemaker, XKool also sees its AI-based technology not as a replacement of the architect but rather as an 'AI assistant', a prosthetic extension to empower the architect. The idea is to hand over the routine and repetitive work to the computer – work that the computer is probably capable of doing faster and more accurately – so as to leave the architect more time to devote to the creative process. The role of AI here is to tirelessly adapt to the ever-changing requirements of the design process, and to come up with informed suggestions. As He notes, 'There is no doubt that future cities will still be created by the human will, but in a different way, empowered by technologies.'[29]

Unlike Spacemaker, however, Xkool focuses on deep learning. Its objective is to streamline the design process and make it more efficient and creative by using deep learning to not only search through a vast range of possibilities, but also automatically generate designs based on the trained models, and then evaluate and return the outcomes from various evaluation models. In effect, Xkool uses generative adversarial networks (GANs) to produce a range of potential solutions. It can also take account of site conditions and environmental factors so as to evaluate possible outcomes and identify the best potential solution.

The story of Xkool can be understood as a story of constantly evolving design processes. He and Yang first used AI back in 2011 in an entry for the international competition for the Shenzhen Bay Eco-Tech City, which subsequently became one of the first AI-assisted designs to be actually built. The breakthrough came, however, when they developed a GAN-based technique involving a 'design brain' and an 'evaluation brain' with the formation of Xkool in 2016. Broadly put, the role of the 'design brain' was to generate a range of possible design solutions based on a massive dataset of previous designs. The role of the 'evaluation brain' was to evaluate and rank these designs based on land value and other local data. In effect, the 'design brain' and the 'evaluation brain' worked together, with the 'design brain' generating possible designs, and the 'evaluation brain' evaluating them.[30]

This first set of tools, however, had their limitations. Although useful in speeding up the design process and reducing costs, they did not provide sufficient 'references' to be really practical.[31] The situation was helped with improvements in machine learning that Xkool subsequently incorporated into its working method.[32] This led to the launch of Xkool's 'Rosetta Stone' research initiative, so called because it looked at the possibility of generating a range of design outcomes based on different styles of architecture, where these styles were seen as the equivalent of different languages.[33] They then developed a large database of different design styles, based on material extracted from previous architectural designs.

The real advance, however, came as a result of the success of the AlphaGo ZERO initiative. Xkool developed a new technique using reinforcement learning that meant they did not need to rely on datasets of existing buildings. Instead the system was capable of extracting its own rules from previous examples, and generating options that were genuinely innovative and creative:

> In 2017, the official publication of AlphaGo ZERO showed research results that promoted the application of reinforcement learning technology in developing intelligent design tools. It freed design tools from the limitations of the database of real cases towards a direct use of initial models generated by rules they have learnt in confrontation and iteration. By repeating this process, a model that best meets (or even exceeds) human designers' expectations and has a true potential for exploring the unknown is finally generated.[34]

In their latest stage of development, Xkool now sees the role of AI as being broken down into four distinct stages: recognition, evaluation, reconstruction and generation.[35] 'Recognition' is used to search for complex and hidden patterns in the data generated by cities. Of course, humans are also capable of recognising patterns, but the sheer amount of data makes it impossible for them to do so effectively, and there are often 'blind spots' in any analysis undertaken by humans. The next step, 'evaluation', involves detecting patterns in this data, such as pedestrian movement or traffic flow. This can help to reveal problems such as traffic congestion or a lack of public facilities.[36]

After that comes 'reconstruction', a background process that helps to form a basic understanding of the challenge. For example, the development of this technique allowed Xkool to launch the platform

FIGURE 6.5 Xkool, KoolPlan generated design (2019). KoolPlan is an AI assistant for floor plans and façade design that allows for more refined detailing.

'Non-Existing Architectures' in 2019 that was able to generate relatively convincing 'hallucinations' of buildings based on a massive dataset of building images.[37] Xkool has also developed a technique called AI-chitect for constructing a complete image of a building based on an outline sketch, a technique first displayed in the *Eyes of the City* exhibition in the 2019 Shenzhen Biennale of Urbanism/Architecture.[38] This brings the vision of Xkool closer to the vision of Spacemaker, making AI exceptionally easy to use.

However, reconstruction can only operate at a relatively basic level, to produce little more than impressionistic designs. It therefore depends on the final step, 'generation', to provide a more detailed and refined output. 'Generation' is similar to the process of turning a rough sketch into a detailed design. Xkool has developed two tools for this. Firstly, on an urban scale, they have developed their 'Intelligent Dynamic Urban Planning and Decision-Making Platform', an integrated dynamic platform which allows the overall plan for urban planning proposals to be modified, as each component part is itself modified. This platform has already been used in the planning of Xiong'an New Area, an urban development in the Beijing-Tainjin-Hebei economic triangle. Secondly, on an architectural scale, they have developed their 'AI Design Cloud Platform'. As the name implies, this platform operates through the cloud and does not require any software to be installed.

The latest development in this platform has been the introduction of Koolplan, an AI assistant to generate more detailed floor plans and elevations. Koolplan offers designers a range of possible options from which to choose their preferred solution, a significant improvement on earlier shape grammar techniques that only offer designers a single solution.[39] Xkool is now not far from developing a fully automated process for generating actual architectural drawings.

Spacemaker v Xkool

Spacemaker and Xkool were both launched in 2016. Both claim to be the first company in the world to develop an AI-assisted platform for architectural design and construction. Both have a particular focus on property development. Both have attracted significant funding. And both believe that – for the moment at any rate – the architect still plays an important role in the design process. But are they in fact so similar?

When it comes to comparing Spacemaker and Xkool, many factors need to be taken into account. For example, Spacemaker caters primarily for a Western market, whereas Xkool technology is currently available only in China.[40] But when comparing the two companies, we need to examine exactly how they operate. After all, it is not always obvious how much AI is involved, or indeed what kind of AI. There is, for example, a significant difference between GOFAI techniques, such as topological optimisation, and deep learning.

Although Spacemaker uses AI, it also uses a range of other technologies. As Maria Dantz comments, AI is not necessarily the main driver of their processes, as least as far as their customers are concerned:

> Our current website is very much about an AI centered platform, but AI is just one part of the entire platform. A big part of what our users actually like are the analyses. It's the analytics. It's being able to use data in a way that they weren't able to use and combine data before, in a model. And then you can basically integrate that with the optimisation of plans and the AI part. So that is just one aspect, but it's not necessarily the driver for every one of our customers.[41]

In contrast, Xkool makes extensive use of machine learning, especially deep learning, although the company leaves open the opportunity for human intervention with KoolPlan and other features. The problem with deep learning, of course, is that it consumes vast amounts of data. But this is where Xkool has something of an advantage, in that it obtains its data from local clients and collaborators, such as real estate developers, legal urban data suppliers and government companies. Indeed, China produces significantly more data than any country and has fewer concerns about privacy issues. As has been observed, 'If data is the new oil, China is the new OPEC.'[42]

Importantly, Xkool also obtains data from data-labelling companies. China's fast growing AI industries cannot do without high-quality and well-labelled learning data that is highly specified and targeted for specific applications. Although open-source, labelled data is available from other countries, but is still unsuitable for specific applications. For example, labelled housing data from Japan is incompatible with China's housing market. However, Chinese 'data farms', the equivalent of Amazon's 'Mechanical Turk', are capable of supplying compatible data for specific applications. This is the new industry that is silently supporting AI start-ups and enterprises in China.

Although they are not in direct competition, it would be interesting to see whether Xkool's investment in deep learning gives it an

FIGURE 6.6 Xkool is a cloud-based AI design platform that is becoming very popular with both architects and developers.

advantage. Or will Spacemaker's use of a range of tools in addition to AI make its platform easier to control and more user-friendly? And what will happen to Spacemaker now that it has been acquired by Autodesk? Only time will tell.

Redesigning design

It is worth reflecting on how computation in general and AI in particular have changed how we operate these days. For example, how do we go about writing an essay or article in the age of Google? Chances are that we will start by making a Google search of a few key words associated with the subject matter. This is how we access knowledge these days. The astonishing improvement in the speed of search engines over the past few years has meant that within a fraction of a second we can search all available information online. As such, the traditional method of 'browsing' through books in a library has now become if not totally redundant, then at least downgraded to a recreational pastime.

Or how do we take photos in the age of the digital photography? In the old days of manual photography we would carefully set up the camera for one ideal shot. In the age of digital photography, however, we take a burst of *sample* shots. We then review them, select our favourite shot and enhance it using editing techniques available on every smart phone. It is no longer a question of the expert photographer setting up the ideal shot, but rather of the informed user taking an array of *sample* photos and then selecting and enhancing the best one.

In the age of AI, this process of 'sampling' or 'searching' has also become the first step in the design process. Instead of developing a single design, the tendency now is to define the constraints and conduct a search, in order to generate a range of possible outcomes. With Grasshopper this amounts to writing a definition and adjusting sliders to generate as many options as needed. With AI, a range of options can be generated automatically. The assumption here is that all possible solutions already exist, and that it is simply a question of searching for them:

If we think through the logic of the search in the context of 'design', what such an approach suggests is that if all possible solutions

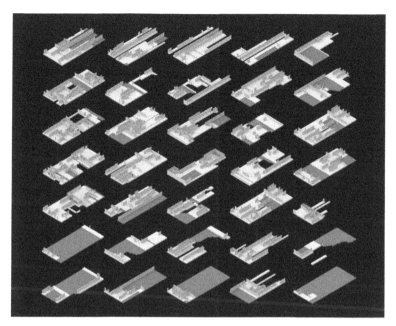

FIGURE 6.7 Immanuel Koh, *Sampling-Mies* (2018). Mies van der Rohe's original 1929 Barcelona Pavilion is shown right in the middle amongst an infinite multitude of newly inferred ones. Each new pavilion retains, with varying degree of fidelity, the formal relationships among voids, walls, columns, steps, ground and furniture of the autoregressively machine-learnt Barcelona Pavilion.

already exist, it is simply a question of defining a set of constraints and conducting a search, and then selecting one of the many outcomes. The potential implications of this are far reaching. Not only does it challenge the traditional notion . . . but it also suggests that if there is still any creativity in the 'design' process, it should lie, firstly, in defining the constraints that generate the range of possible solutions to a problem, and, secondly, in developing an effective method of filtering or evaluating them.[43]

This has major implications for the logic of design itself. The top-down architect form maker of the past gives way to the architect as controller of processes. This shifts the emphasis from the 'creativity' of the designer towards the rigour of the search itself, and challenges the whole notion of the 'creative genius'. However, we can still use our traditional aesthetic sensibilities – our architect's 'eye' – to evaluate the outcomes. Indeed the architect's eye remains one of the most valuable assets in the design process, and can be surprisingly quick at making an evaluation. As a result, we can observe how some architects and designers deploy highly sophisticated software to generate possible solutions, and then simply use their 'eye' to judge the most attractive.[44]

As a corollary to this, we need to rethink the terminology that we use. If the notion of a singular design is being replaced by a range of potential sample options, should we not refer to them as 'outcomes?' And if the notion of designing is to be replaced by a search for possible outcomes, should we not refer to this process as 'searching'? Surely the designer here is merely the instigator of a process, and the result of that process is more of an outcome than a design in the traditional sense.

The introduction of AI into architectural design also allows for a more exhaustive and comprehensive search of the solution space. In the traditional design process we tend to start by thinking about a range of possible solutions. But our own human biases often limit that range.[45] AI, however, helps us to expand the range of solutions.[46] In other words, AI exposes us to solutions that otherwise we would not have thought about.

Interestingly, Larry Page, co-founder of Google, goes so far as to claim that AI aspires to be the ultimate search engine:

Artificial Intelligence would be the ultimate version of Google. The ultimate search engine that would understand everything on the web. It would understand exactly what you wanted, and it would give you the right thing. We're nowhere near doing that now. However, we can get incrementally closer to that, and that is basically what we work on.[47]

'Google, what is the answer to life, the universe and everything?'[48]

In 2018 I was so amazed that almost 90 per cent of my students were writing essays about AI – and good essays, on the whole – that I seriously wondered whether they might have been using an AI programme to generate them. As it happened, the essays had not been generated by AI. But it is now possible for GPT-3 to generate highly convincing texts.[49]

AI, write me an essay.

Eventually the same will also be true for design. Soon we will also generate designs with a simple voice command, and those designs will not only be of the highest standard but they will also completely match our aesthetic preferences.

AI, design me a building.[50]

7

AI and the city of the future

What will the city of the future look like? Will it look strikingly different to cities of today? Will it look like something out of *The Jetsons*, complete with flying cars and space age buildings? Or will it look much like our contemporary cities, with a few new buildings, but with much of the existing building stock retained and simply retrofitted with the latest AI technologies? In other words, will the primary driver of change be a language of novel architectural forms? Or will it be the introduction of ever more sophisticated AI-based technologies?

For Patrik Schumacher the city of the future will consist of novel architectural forms designed using the latest computational tools. In his article in 'Digital Cities', an issue of *Architectural Design* (*AD*) published in 2009, 'Parametricism: A New Global Style for Architecture and Urban Design', Schumacher outlines the design logic of Parametricism, which, he maintains, has now superseded modernism and other contemporary styles as the new global style of architecture. Schumacher begins by describing parametricism as being rooted in advanced computational techniques:

> There is a global convergence in recent avant-garde architecture that justifies its designation as a new style: parametricism. It is a style rooted in digital animation techniques, its latest refinements based on advanced parametric design systems and scripting methods. Developed over the past 15 years and now claiming hegemony within avant-garde architecture practice, it succeeds Modernism as the next long wave of systematic innovation.[1]

FIGURE 7.1 Zaha Hadid Architects, Kartal-Pendik Masterplan, Istanbul, Turkey (2006). The Kartal-Pendik project requires the design of a sub-centre on Istanbul's Asian side to reduce pressure on the city's historic core. The site is being reclaimed from industrial estates and is flanked by the small-grain fabric of suburban towns.

It is a style, moreover, with its own quite recognisable characteristics: 'Aesthetically, it is the elegance of ordered complexity and the sense of seamless fluidity, akin to natural systems that constitute the hallmark of parametricism.'[2] And it is a style that, although it can be expressed at any scale from interior design to urban design, is most effective in large-scale urban developments: 'So pervasive is the application of its techniques that parametricism is now evidenced at all scales from architecture to interior design to large urban design. Indeed, the larger the project, the more pronounced is parametricism's superior capacity to articulate programmatic complexity.'[3] Schumacher illustrates his article with a series of large-scale urban proposals for Istanbul, Singapore and Beijing. For Schumacher, the cities of the future will look decidedly futuristic, and bear the hallmark of parametricism.

It is now more than ten years since the publication of the 'Digital Cities' issue of *AD*, and it is worth enquiring whether any cities designed according to the logic of parametricism have ever been built.[4] Even in China, the one country whose scale of development has exceeded that of most other countries, we can see little evidence of this. Admittedly, there are a number of large-scale housing developments – and even complete cities – that have been built, but none that subscribe to the logic of parametricism. And although collectively the many buildings designed by ZHA across the globe would perhaps constitute an entire city, so far no *individual* city has been designed exclusively according to the logic of parametricism. It is as though developers and policymakers have not been persuaded to adopt novel forms – and novel forms alone – when developing a city.[5]

Nor has there been much evidence of any large-scale developments – progressive or otherwise – in existing cities, such as New York, London, Paris and Moscow. This is for obvious reasons. After all, the plots left vacant in these already established cities are relatively small, and seldom does it makes economic sense to demolish existing buildings to make way for new ones. Moreover, any new development is often constrained by building preservation orders and planning restrictions. In short, renovation, refurbishment and interior redesign are often the preferred strategies in existing cities.

'iPhone City'

In his own contribution to the same issue of *AD*, 'iPhone City', Benjamin Bratton takes a completely different approach.[6] Forget futuristic architectural forms. Think informational processes.[7] Bratton observes that there is an advanced computational device that is already changing our experience of cities: the simple iPhone. Although the iPhone has had little impact as yet on the design of new cities, it has already had a profound impact on how we operate in our existing cities. The development of smart navigation apps, for example, has allowed us to navigate and understand cities in new ways, while the introduction of roaming has allowed the car to become the new office, as a hybrid 'car + phone' platform.[8]

In 2009 the transportation interface Uber was launched as 'UberCab', although the app for mobile phones was not released until the following year. As such, Bratton wrote his essay before Uber came into existence. However, it is worth considering how even more insightful his analysis of the car becoming 'car + office' would have been had he been aware that the domestic car would itself become a potential source of employment. Uber has now spawned a number of competitors, such as Lyft, in a process that has been described as 'uber-ification', and ride sharing apps have now become endemic in major cities throughout the world.[9] In China, companies like DiDi have proved so successful that they have effectively forced Uber out of the market.[10] The secret, as the success of Uber has shown us, is to harness the capacity of informational interfaces to generate new kinds of employment. In other words, computation has not given us new seductive forms, but rather new ways of operating.

This challenges the claim made by architectural historian Mario Carpo, in his book *The Second Digital Turn*, that big data gives us another style of architecture.[11] Carpo argues that the sheer amount of 'messy' data available today has led to a new messy, 'voxelated' style of architecture.[12] Surely this is another example of the problem of 'architecturalisation' – of reading non-architectural concepts as though they are referring to architectural forms.[13] What big data has to do with architectural form remains something of a mystery. Big data relates to information and not to form. Has the introduction of ride-sharing services actually changed the appearance of anything? In fact, if we look at Uber cars themselves, they look identical to ordinary cars. This is because they *are* ordinary cars. Despite what Carpo might claim, big data does not promote any particular aesthetic. It simply allows ride-sharing companies such as Uber to operate in a more effective and efficient manner than the straightforward taxis of the past.

The information architect

In his essay, Bratton includes a provocation, calling for half of all architects to abandon the traditional model of the architect form-maker to effectively become what we might call 'information architects', drawing upon their design skills and computational abilities to develop not new designs, but new software that could be used to rework existing structures and systems:

> An experiment: one half of all architects and urbanists in the entire world should, as of now, stop designing new buildings and new developments altogether. Instead they should invest the historical

depth and intellectual nuance of their architectural imaginations into the design and programming of new software that provides for the better use of structures and systems we already have. It is a simple matter of good content management. The other half, the control group, may continue as before.[14]

One architect who has seemingly risen to the challenge to become an 'information architect' is Shan He. Trained as an architect at Tsinghua University and MIT, she was the founder of Uber's data visualisation team, where she developed Uber's kepler.gl software. Since then she has set up her own geospatial analytics and visualisation company, Unfolded.[15]

For He, big data does not change the forms that we design, as Carpo seems to believe, but the way that we design. 'How is big data changing the way we design cities?' asks He.[16] For some time now, architects and urban planners have been using ESRI and other data mining techniques to inform their designs, but it is the sheer quantities of data available and the range of new tools and techniques that is providing so much more information to inform designs:

FIGURE 7.2 Shan He, UK Commute, map of commuting patterns in England and Wales in Unfolded studio. The map visualises commuting patterns within England and Wales based on the 2011 Census. It contains 679,000 commute connections, visualised using Unfolded studio. Each arc connects the place people live the place they work.

Rapid developments in spatial data-mining, analytics and visualisation mean that urbanists now have a collection of open data, advanced tooling and analytic models at hand to tackle complex urban issues. Granted geospatial data have always been used in the planning process to facilitate decision making, but it is the explosive volume, variety and resolution of it, alongside increasing analytic capacity, that has fundamentally changed the horizon of urban studies.[17]

But He is not asking architects and urban designers to completely abandon their traditional skill set. Rather, she is calling on them to adopt a hybrid approach, much like the 'extended intelligence' model outlined above. Here technology becomes an extension of the designer's imagination, empowering the designer of the future:

> A city is not only a machine that delivers goods and services; it is a place that facilitates human experiences. Urban designers need the basic skills to achieve both these functions, to use data as a means of designing sustainable cities while at the same time using their craftsmanship to create enchanting city forms.[18]

Bratton's essay has proved to be extraordinarily insightful. The future city, for Bratton, cannot be based on innovative forms alone. It also needs to embrace new informational systems. And we need to rethink the logic of architectural practice, shifting away from the all but exclusive model of the architect form-maker of the past, and opening up to also embrace a new model of the 'information architect'. In hindsight, Bratton's essay on the impact of new technologies on our cities stands out as by far the most perspicacious in the entire 'Digital Cities' volume.

The informational city

The idea of the informational city is not new. Manuel Castells published the book *The Informational City: Information Technology, Economic Restructuring and the Urban-Regional Process* back in 1989.[19] Castells followed this up with a trilogy of books on 'the information age', where he celebrates the 'network society', which operates not through integrated hierarchies but through organisational networks, and which depends upon the constant flow of information through technology.[20]

More recently, we have seen the development of the 'smart city', equipped, as Michael Batty comments, with 'constellations of instruments across many scales that are connected through multiple networks which provide continuous data regarding the movements of people and materials and the status of various structures and system'.[21] Batty adds, however, that in order to be smart these systems need to be integrated into an effective whole, so as to provide some overall benefit: 'Cities however can only be smart if there are intelligence functions that are able to integrate and synthesise this data to some purpose, ways of improving the efficiency, equity, sustainability and quality of life in cities.'[22]

More recently still, Bratton has published *The Stack*, where he extends the model of the networked society and the smart city.[23] Instead of being limited to a single horizontal layer, Bratton describes the networked society in terms of a vertical aggregation of horizontal

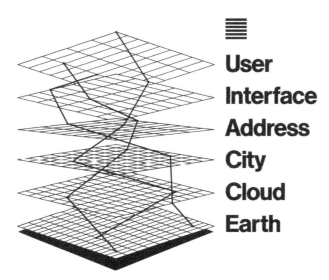

User
Interface
Address
City
Cloud
Earth

FIGURE 7.3 Diagram by Metahaven of the six layers of the Stack. Benjamin Bratton, *The Stack*, Cambridge, MA: MIT Press, 2015.

layers. Bratton therefore extends Castell's 2D model to 3D space.[24] And instead of seeing the various forms of planetary scale computing as differentiated components, Bratton sees them as layers of a consolidated metaplatform that takes the form of an 'accidental megastructure'. Bratton refers to this as 'The Stack':

> The Stack refers to a transformation in the technical infrastructure of global systems, whereby planetary-scale computation has so thoroughly transformed the logics of political geography in its own image that it has produced new geographies and new territories that can enforce themselves. Unlike modern political geography, which divided up horizontal maps, Stack geography also vertically layers spaces on top of one another. Instead of surveying all the various forms of planetary-scaled computation – cloud computing, smart cities, ubiquitous computing, massive addressing systems, next-generation interfaces, nonhuman users, and so on – as different genres or species of computing, each off on its own, this model locates them on layers of a consolidated metaplatform, an accidental megastructure.[25]

The Stack is composed of six layers: the *Earth* layer, *Cloud* layer, *City* layer, *Address* layer, *Interface* layer and *User* layer. The *Earth* layer 'provides a physical foundation for the Stack; the *Cloud* layer consists of 'vast server archipelagos'; the *City* layer 'comprises the environment of discontinuous megacities and meganetworks'; the *Address* layer 'examines massively granular universal addressing systems'; the *Interface* layer provides 'imagistic and linguistic mediation between *Users* and the *Addressable* computational capacities of their habitats'; and finally the *User* layer includes both human and non-human users.[26]

The key here is connectivity. The Stack represents the interconnected, informational pathways around the world today in terms of either vertical or horizontal interfaces, where each layer constitutes not a discrete separation but a form of connectivity with other layers; the *City* layer, for example, might interact with the next vertical – the *Cloud* layer or the *Earth* layer – or indeed it might skip a layer and interface with the *Earth* layer, or it might interface with another city on the same layer. Likewise, a city can also be understood as a city within a global network of cities. Whether we refer to the 'informational city', the 'smart city' or the 'city layer' of the stack, however, it is clear that cities of today are becoming the sites of informational interfaces, where AI and AI-based apps are playing an increasing role.

Ambient intelligence

The impact of AI on the city does not need to be viewed at the scale of the overall city. Indeed, the secret to understanding the city, as Jane Jacobs reminds us, is to perceive it in terms not of top-down major changes, such as master planning, but of incremental behaviours at a street level.[27] The city could therefore be understood as constituted by a multiplicity of users, no less than flocks of birds or schools of fish are constituted by individual agents. The city might be significantly larger in scale than individual agents, but the city is constituted precisely by individual agents. In this way, we can understand that the city is already populated with AI-informed devices. After all, as Bratton astutely observes, the city *wears us*, as much as we ourselves wear our devices.[28] By extension, the city itself can be understood as wearing our intelligent devices. Meanwhile Bratton's notion of the Stack highlights the interconnected operations. In the informational city of today, intelligence is fast becoming pervasive through the medium of the individual inhabitants and their personal AI-informed devices.

We live in a world of 'seamless intelligent devices' that are sensitive and responsive to occupants, and not dependent on manual control. Another way to describe this landscape of interconnected devices is as a space of 'ambient intelligence (AmI)'.[29] The spaces in which we now live conform less to Le Corbusier's notion of 'a machine for living in' and more to Mark Weiser's notion of 'ubiquitous computing'.[30] Soon we will not even need to carry our devices around with us. Computation will be seamlessly embedded in the urban environment, as freely available as the air that we breathe, and we will be able to communicate with our environment through speech and gestures.[31] With this shift, as technology is absorbed within the fabric of the city itself, life in the city is no longer dominated by

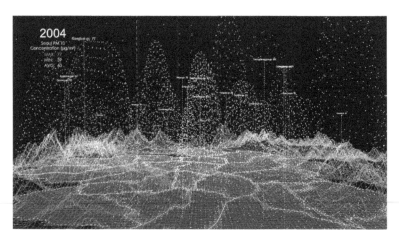

FIGURE 7.4 Zhenwei Zhong and Chuhan Zhou, *Approaching Convergence* (2017). A project visualising the Particulate Matter 10 (PM10) data of Seoul acquired from the weather stations in twenty-five districts, for the 'Approaching Convergance' course at Columbia GSAPP, co-taught by Biayna Bogosian and Maider Llaguno-Munitxa.

explicit forms of computation. The environment itself would become intelligent.

We could even imagine this intelligent environment responding interactively to our moods and comfort levels. It would be able to stimulate us when lethargic, and soothe us when agitated;[32] cool us down when hot, and warm us up when cold. It would become an adaptive, sympathetic, nurturing environment of ambient intelligence, responsive to our individual needs.

Of course, there are potentially negative consequences too. We could imagine that such an environment would be quite capable of tracking our every move and monitoring our behaviour. It would also be capable, no doubt, of bombarding us with customised advertisements. We should not overlook, then, the dark side of AmI. In the wrong hands, it could be highly detrimental.[33] At the same time, however, we should avoid the technological determinism that is often associated with negative attitudes towards technology.[34] No technology is inherently bad.[35] Used in the right way, AmI can be highly beneficial to society.

Swarm intelligence

In *Emergence: The Collective Lives of Ants, Brains, Cities and Software*, Steven Johnson outlines the theory of emergence.[36] To be clear, Johnson is not the first to mention this theory, and is greatly indebted to the work of others, but the success of his book has done much to popularise the theory of emergence.[37]

Emergence can be observed wherever two or more agents interact in a bottom-up manner.[38] But it is most evident in a multi-agent system whose interaction leads to a global behaviour. As the subtitle of the book suggests, Johnson makes an explicit connection between the emergent behaviours of a range of multi-agent systems – such as ants, brains, cities and software – no matter

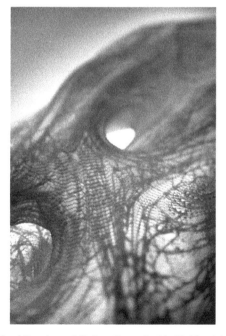

FIGURE 7.5 Roland Snooks and Robert Stuart-Smith (Kokkugia) in collaboration with Studio Pei Zhu, National Art Museum of China (NAMOC) (2013). The form was generated through a swarm-based algorithm – developed from the turbulent and chaotic systems underlying cloud formation.

how incommensurable their constituent elements.[39] We can therefore make direct comparisons between the operations of a city and the behaviour of a brain.[40]

Emergence has become a highly popular term in recent architectural discourse, but it is worth recalling that the term itself does not necessarily refer to contemporary design issues.[41] On the contrary, it could be argued that emergence can be viewed most clearly in traditional urban formations. For it is precisely the less self-conscious forms of urban aggregation that characterise the development of traditional settlements, from medieval villages to Chinese hutongs or Brazilian favelas, that fits best the simple rules of emergence, such as 'ignorance is useful' or 'pay attention to your neighbours'. These forms of urbanism constitute a relatively homogeneous field of operations, where individual components do not stand out but conform to the pervasive logic of their surrounding environment.

Another way to think about emergence is through the logic of swarm intelligence. This is expressed in the decentralised, self-organising behaviour of multi-agent systems.[42] As Roland Snooks observes, 'Swarm Intelligence operates through the local interaction of autonomous agents that gives rise to emergent collective behavior within decentralised self-organising systems.'[43] An everyday example of 'swarm intelligence' can be observed when a flock of birds, such as starlings, comes in to roost in the evening. The complex aerial gymnastics of these birds are defined not by any top-down logic imposed from above, but rather by a bottom-up logic that 'emerges' out of the simple interactions between the individual birds. As the flock swoops, soars or veers in any direction, it is not being directed or controlled by any one particular bird. Rather, each individual bird is following a certain set of basic rules related to principles of cohesion, separation and alignment – keeping a certain distance from the birds in front and on all sides, while flying at the same speed and travelling in the same basic direction – and it is this that dictates the overall behaviour of the flock.

Importantly, however, a collective intelligence arises out of these individual behaviours that is not predetermined and fixed, but self-regulating and adaptive: 'Constantly mutating, emergent systems are intelligent systems, based on interaction, informational feedback loops, pattern recognition and indirect control. They challenge the

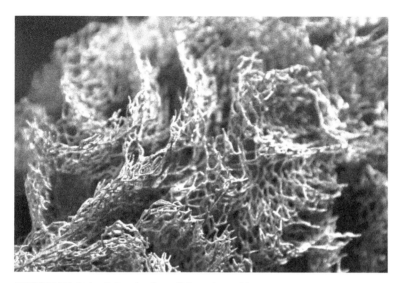

FIGURE 7.6 Roland Snooks (in collaboration with Scott Mayson), *RMIT Mace* (2015). The mace was designed using a multi-agent system, and 3D printed using a laser sintering process that fuses titanium powder to create a highly intricate and lightweight structure.

traditional conception of systems as predetermined mechanisms of control, and focus instead on their self-regulating adaptive capacity.'[44] The intelligence exhibited in these displays of swarm intelligence, might be a relatively low level form of intelligence – such as the intelligence of slime mould foraging for food – but it is a form of intelligence nonetheless. Swarm intelligence can be understood as a basic form of AI.

Progressive architectural culture is constantly in search of novel architectural forms. It is therefore no surprise that the logic of the swarm has been increasingly appropriated by experimental practices as a referential metaphor and an organisational analog for embracing complexity and developing non-linear design methodologies that operate through multi-agent algorithms. Architects such as Snooks and Alisa Andrasek have used Processing for generating such forms, while others, such as Daniel Bolojan, have written their own multi-agent software programmes. These systems are certainly capable of generating attractive and strikingly novel forms.[45] As such, they have had a significant influence on architectural design culture.

Once a multi-agent system has been frozen into a static architectural form, however, its complex behaviours are necessarily curtailed and its full potential unrealised.[46] And yet, as Deleuze and Guattari have observed, a city should be understood as 'deterritorialised' rather than 'territorialised', smooth rather than striated. It is a function of dynamic circulations and circuits, and can never be reduced to a singular, static form:

> The town is the correlate of the road. The town exists only as a function of circulation and of circuits; it is a singular point on the circuits which create it and which it creates. It is defined by entries and exits: something must enter it and exit from it. It imposes a frequency. It effects a polarization of matter, inert, living or human; it causes the phylum, the flow, to pass through specific places, along horizontal lines. It is a phenomenon of transconsistency, a network, because it is fundamentally in contact with other towns. It represents a threshold of deterritorialization because whatever the material involved, it must be deterritorialized enough to enter the network, to submit to the polarization, to follow the circuit of urban and road recoding.[47]

Arguably, then, we can glimpse the potential of swarm intelligence informing the logic of the city if we focus less on the static buildings and more on the dynamic behaviour of agents within a city. A city, after all, can never be reduced to a collection of buildings. A city is nothing without its inhabitants. We need to distinguish between a city as a site of material deposits – as an amalgam of traces of construction – and a city as the site of spatial practices. The former can be read in terms of an accretion of material deposits that form the built environment, and the latter can be read in terms of choreographies of human agents whose freedom of movement is constrained by that environment.[48] The city, then, is constituted not only by physical buildings but also by human agents, and must be understood as a human–mineral hybrid system. This has major implications for how we can understand the impact of swarm intelligence on the city.

In his book, *Out of Control: The New Biology of Machines, Social Systems, and the Economic World*, Kevin Kelly has extended the principle of swarm intelligence and shown how it can also offer us a convincing model for dynamic behaviour of the economy, in that the economy itself also operates in a bottom-up, out-of-control fashion.[49] As one customer copies the purchasing habits of another customer – much like a bird following another bird in a flock or an ant following a pheromone trail – consumer patterns begin to emerge, so that the purchasing habits of individual customers appear as a collective whole. These behaviours, however, are bottom-up, based on individual choices. They are not controlled from above in any way. The market, then, is potentially volatile – 'out of control' – and fuelled by trends.

With the real estate market, these trends become spatialised across the fabric of the city. Certain businesses begin to cluster together in particular districts of the city, as one business owner follows the example of other business owners. Likewise, as the popularity of certain neighbourhoods begins to wax and wane, certain districts come into vogue and others fall out of favour. Understood in these terms, the economic behaviour of our cities could be compared to the operations of a meteorological system. As registers of popularity and appeal begin to shift and mutate over the fabric of the city, like high and low pressure systems, they generate an undulating economic landscape, creating points of intensity, but also zones of depression, reflected in real-estate values. Seen in this light, the entire city is governed by the logic of the swarm.

The self-regulating city

John Holland describes how the city somehow manages to maintain a form of dynamic equilibrium, despite the constant changes that it experiences. He likens it to a 'standing wave' in a stream. A city can be seen as a 'pattern in time':

> Cities have no central planning commissions that solve the problem of purchasing and distributing supplies . . . How do these cities avoid devastating swings between shortage and glut, year after year, decade after decade? The mystery deepens when we observe the kaleidoscopic nature of large cities. Buyers, sellers, administrations, streets, bridges, and buildings are always changing, so that a city's coherence is somehow imposed on a perpetual flux of people and

structures. Like the standing wave in front of a rock in a fast-moving stream, the city is a pattern in time.[50]

After all, according to the logic of emergence, cities are physical traces of patterns of social behaviour operating over time. They are governed by principles of self-organisation. For cities and towns themselves must be understood as amalgams of 'processes', as spaces of vectorial flows that 'adjust' to differing inputs and impulses, like some self-regulating system. But how does a city manage to maintain this equilibrium?[51] Could the model of the 'city as brain' help us to understand this mechanism?

The brain, as we know, does more than just think. It also serves to regulate the body. This mechanism is often referred to as 'homeostasis'.[52] Homeostasis (or homoeostasis) is the property of a system that maintains a constant equilibrium when faced with internal or external variables. It is a concept that has been used in a number of fields including biology, mechanical systems and – more recently – in the field of neuroscience. In the context of neuroscience, homeostasis can here be understood as a kind of equilibrium on which the body depends for its survival.

William Ross Ashby, one of the pioneers in cybernetics and author of *Design for a Brain*, developed a device that he called the 'homeostat', a balancing mechanism – much like a thermostat – that maintains some kind of equilibrium through negative feedback.[53] The purpose of this device was to model the way in which the brain achieves its own form of dynamic equilibrium.[54] Significantly, Ashby's work caught the attention of Alan Turing, who wrote to him suggesting that he use his Automatic Computing Engine (ACE) to simulate the process rather than building a special machine. In his letter to Ashby, Turing confessed, 'I am more interested in producing models of the action of the brain, than in the practical applications of computing.'[55] With this, the connection between homeostasis, computation and the operations of the brain had been established.

More recently, neuroscientist Antonio Damasio has argued that the primary function of the brain is to maintain our homeostatic condition and preserve our dynamic psychic equilibrium.[56] Thus the brain can be seen to operate less as a 'command control center' and more as a corrective mechanism that keeps the body within a safe range of emotional impulses. As Damasio comments, 'Survival depends on the maintenance of the body's physiology within an optimal homeostatic range. This process relies on fast detection of potentially deleterious changes in body state and on appropriate corrective responses.'[57] While the brain itself is highly adaptive, it can also serve as a mechanism of adaptation.

The self-organisation of cities can therefore be compared to the dynamic equilibrium of the brain. After all, cities are governed by both positive and negative feedback, much like the brain itself. At a very basic level, then, we can see parallels between Damasio's understanding of the homeostasis of the brain and the principles of self-organisation that underpin a city which could be reflected potentially in the behaviour of any multi-agent system, such as a neural network.

'Brains and cities, it would seem, have much in common.'

Could the city be understood literally *as* a brain? In strict neuroscientific terms, it obviously could not be. One is a human–mineral hybrid system, and one a biological organism.[58] Nonetheless a city could be described as a *kind* of brain, albeit perhaps not a human brain. Brains and cities, it would seem, have much in common.[59] Both are multi-agent systems. The same could be said of certain software systems. A neural network, after all, is composed of individual neurons which contribute to an emergent collective behaviour. As Kelleher comments:

> The overall behavior of the network emerges from the interactions of the processing carried out by individual neurons within the network. Neural networks solve problems using a divide-and-conquer strategy: each of the neurons in a network solves one component of a larger problem, and the overall problem is solved by combining these component solutions.[60]

This means that we can extend the paradigm of emergence from relatively dumb creatures, such as ants, to the sophistication of the brain, and on to cities and the operations of neural networks themselves. The opportunity therefore presents itself for using neural networks to model – and potentially augment – the operations of a city as a form of brain.

'City Brain'

Perhaps the most extensive exploration of the application of AI to the city has been the 'City Brain' initiative developed by Alibaba, a leading Chinese ecommerce company at the forefront of machine-learning development.[61] City Brain is effectively a 'digital twin' of the city itself. The idea behind the City Brain project is to develop a cloud-based system that stores information about the city in real time and uses machine learning to process that information in order to control the operations of the city and improve its performance. Liu Feng, one of the computer scientists behind the City Brain project, offers us a definition of the City Brain:

> The City Brain is a new architecture of the Smart City based on the model of the Internet Brain. Under the support of the city central nervous system (cloud computing), the city sensory nervous system (Internet of Things), the city motor nervous system (Industry 4.0, Industrial Internet) and the city nerve endings (Edge Computing), a city can achieve the human–human, human–things and things–things information interaction through the city neural network (Big SNS) and achieve the rapid smart response to city services through the city cloud reflex arcs, so as to promote the organic integration of all components of a city, realizing the continuous progress of city wisdom. Such a brain-like smart city architecture is called 'City Brain'.[62]

Initially, the City Brain initiative focused solely on traffic in the city of Hangzhou, where Alibaba is based, understandably perhaps, given that Hangzhou used to suffer some of the worst traffic problems in China.[63] It has proved surprisingly effective in improving the operational efficiency of the city. A pilot study showed that City Brain could increase the speed of traffic by 15 per cent and detect illegal parking. Moreover, by constantly monitoring traffic in the city it can detect any signs of a potential collision or accident and by detecting accidents and alerting the police, thereby improving emergency response times.[64] Moreover, by adjusting traffic lights in real time, it can help ambulances and other emergency vehicles reach their destinations more quickly, and prevent traffic congestion during the rush hour.[65] Alibaba claims that City Brain allows ambulances to arrive at their destination seven minutes earlier on average, customers to check in and out of hotels in thirty seconds, and drivers to pass through any pay station in an average time of 2.7 seconds.[66] By keeping the traffic flowing, City Brain therefore serves to maintain the homeostatic condition of the city.[67]

Further versions have since been introduced in nine other cities in China and twenty-three cities worldwide, including Kuala Lumpur, Malaysia.[68] Alibaba is now increasing the range of applications of City Brain, to cover issues such as public transportation, water and energy management, construction activities and public security issues.[69]

Internet–city–brain

The concept of the 'Internet of Things' (IoT) refers to the idea that devices can be interconnected wirelessly. But what would happen if our AI-informed devices were not just connected through the IoT, but *intelligently* connected, like the neurons in the brain? In other words, what if we were to combine the IoT with AI to produce what has been termed the artificial Internet of Things (AIoT)?[70] Would this produce a system that would operate somewhat like the brain?

Some, such as Demis Hassabis, have compared the brain to a computer: 'The brain is just a computer like any other . . . Traits previously considered innate to human – imagination, creativity and even consciousness – may be just the equivalent of software programs.'[71] In fact some scientists claim to have found mini-computers in the neurons of the brain.[72] Others, however, disagree, and argue that the brain is more like the internet than a computer.[73]

As Jeffrey Stibel observes, 'The brain functions very differently from computers, but it functions in a manner similar to the way that the Internet works.'[74] Whereas the computer merely represents a system of neurons, the internet *operates* as a brain.[75] The hardware of the internet is composed of millions of computers all connected in a manner not dissimilar to how neurons in the brain are themselves interconnected, while the software is effectively the web itself.

When I look at Google and the other search engines, I see more similarity to how memories are stored and retrieved in the mind than I do to the underlying computer architecture. When I look at websites, I think memes and memories, not hypertext. When I look at Classmates.com, MySpace, and Facebook, I see social networks that are developing the way neural networks develop, a way that is different than Metcalfe's Law of Networks.

When I look at Internet computing clouds, I see the beginnings of a parallel processing machine that has the ability to go beyond brute calculations, toward the loopy random prediction power of the brain. But as I look out further into the future – as the electronic neurons multiply – I see in cyberspace a replication of biological growth itself, like the evolutionary growth of the brain of an insect, or an animal or even a human being.[76]

Recent neuroscientific research would seem to support this comparison. According to neuroscientists Saket Narlakha and Jonathan Suen, the internet and the brain are not only structured in the same way, but also operate in a similar way:[77]

While the brain and the Internet clearly operate using very different mechanisms, both use simple local rules that give rise to stability. I was initially surprised that biological neural networks utilized the same algorithms as their engineered counterparts, but, as we learned, the requirements for efficiency, robustness, and simplicity are common to both living organisms and networks we have built.[78]

Once we reach this stage, we could expand our comparison between the city and the brain. It is not simply that the city displays a form of self-regulating intelligence, much like the brain. Rather, once the

FIGURE 7.7 ecoLogicStudio with Innsbruck University and UCL Bartlett, *Deep Green*. This project is a reinterpretation of the municipal waste collection networks of Guatemala City using the GAN_Physarum algorithm, whose training is based on Physarum Polycephalum behaviour.

various sensors and devices in a city are connected to form an 'artificial Internet of Things' (AIoT), they will be locked into the secondary logic of an overall system that shares further similarities with the brain.[79]

Whether or not we can make literal comparisons between the city and the brain, it is clear that the city shares certain characteristics with the brain. Both display a form of intelligence. It is important to point out, moreover, that there is no universal definition of 'intelligence'. The intelligence of the city might not match the intelligence of the brain, but it is a form of intelligence nonetheless, just as the swarm intelligence of a slime mould is a form of intelligence.[80]

How, then, are we to understand the intelligence of the AI assisted city? As Wang Jiang comments, 'With the evolution of the city, the city has its own intelligence. It's not artificial intelligence. So, you can't put human intelligence into a city. The city is going to have its own intelligence . . . The city is going to start its own thinking.'[81]

It could be argued, however, that the city already has a form of intelligence – although possibly not the capacity to actually 'think' – through the logic of swarm intelligence. As such, AI can be seen to

FIGURE 8.1 Behnaz Farahi, *Living Breathing Wall* (2013). The movement of this wall is activated by the human voice detected by a Kinect apparatus. The signal then passes through an Arduino control panel to activate a series of Stepper motors.

What predictions, then, have human beings made about the future of AI? Many predictions about AI could be described as mere extrapolations based on existing weak signals and emerging trends. In *Machines that Think: The Future of Artificial Intelligence*, for example, Toby Walsh offers a series of predictions about the year 2050, many of which appear quite straightforward. Walsh predicts that cybercrime will become a major problem, that our health will be monitored by our phones, and that news will be generated by AI. He also predicts that we will talk to our buildings, which is hardly much of a prediction, in that we already do through Alexa and other devices. In short, perhaps the most surprising aspect about some of Walsh's predictions is how unsurprising they are.

Some of his other predictions, however, are perhaps less obvious. Walsh predicts, for example, that we will be able to 'live on' after our deaths through a personalised AI chatbot: 'It will talk like you, it will know the story of your past, it will comfort your family after you die.'[6] Walsh's most interesting prediction, however, relates to the future of driving. He predicts that driving will eventually be banned, as a result of the introduction of self-driving cars.[7] As self-driving cars become more available, Walsh argues, we will drive less and less. As a consequence, our driving skills will diminish, so that insurance premiums will increase. Gradually, we will become resigned to not driving, to the point that young people might not even bother to learn to drive. Finally, driving itself will be banned.

Change, of course, is often incremental, just as the development of the self-driving car is happening gradually over time. In the case of a Tesla car, for example, this takes the form of regular software updates.[8] What is perhaps most interesting about Walsh's prediction, however, is his comment about our change of attitudes: 'We won't be allowed to drive cars any more, and we will not notice or even care.'[9] Human beings are good at adaptation to technologies, but what is often overlooked is the change in social attitudes that result from this adaptation. In a culture of pervasive amnesia, as Andreas Huyssen has described our current epoch, it is remarkable how quickly we forget what life was like in the past.[10] How many of us even remember what life was really like in the days before the internet and mobile phones?

But what if we were to push the implications of some of Walsh's ideas still further? Walsh, for example, predicts that by 2050 we will talk to our rooms. This is hardly much of a prediction in that many of us already talk to our rooms through Alexa, while researchers, such as Behnaz Farahi have developed walls that respond to human speech.[11] Meanwhile both Haley and Kurzweil have already predicted that we will talk to our computers. But what if we were to think through the consequences of the increasing use of voice commands? Would we not start to privilege speech increasingly over writing, once speech-based informational systems have become sufficiently advanced? Would pens, pencils and even keyboards go out of fashion?

We might also surmise that language itself will change with the increasing popularity of speech recognition systems, just as writing changed with the introduction of texting. Speech, after all, is quite different to writing. Anyone who has transcribed a spoken conversation will surely vouch for this. It is remarkable how often, when speaking, people fail to complete a sentence, branching off mid-sentence to a different topic, much like L-systems in computation, and yet still somehow managing to make sense. Moreover, rhetorical strategies, such as calculated pauses, intonation, increase in volume, oratorical flourishes or repetition to reinforce a point – strategies that resonate in spoken language – are lost in writing. As William Hazlitt observes, 'The most dashing orator I ever heard is the flattest writer I ever read.'[12]

But what if we were to combine this insight with Walsh's prediction about self-driving cars? What would be the impact on literacy? Would standards of literacy gradually diminish with the increasing use of speech-based information systems, just as driving skills might diminish with the advent of self-driving cars? Would we gradually lose our ability to even spell, just as neat handwriting declined with the advent of the keyboard? Indeed, let us not forget that in the fourteenth century 80 per cent of English adults were not even able to spell their names, and prior to the development of the printing press, only 30 per cent of European adults were literate.[13] And, if we were to gradually lose the capacity to write, would we even notice or care?

FIGURE 8.2 Behnaz Farahi, *Can the Subaltern Speak?* (2020). These overtly political masks begin to develop their own language to communicate with each other, blinking their multiple eyelashes in rapid succession using a Markov Chain generated Morse code. The work evokes the story of Facebook AI bots that – unnervingly – were thought to have generated their own language, and is intended to illustrate how women could develop their own language to destabilise the authority of patriarchy.

What if we were to push the implications of this even further? What if Haley is correct, and we start to design using voice commands and hand gestures, instead of by drawing? Would drawing go out of fashion? And what if, as a consequence, we were to gradually lose our capacity to draw? And if so, again, would we even notice or care?

Kurzweil's predictions

If there is anyone who has made a name for himself by going out on a limb with often seemingly outrageous predictions, it is surely Ray Kurzweil. His predictions, nonetheless, about technology in general and AI in particular have proved to be remarkably accurate. Indeed, Kurzweil himself claims that 86 per cent of his predictions have been correct.[14]

Although he acknowledges that many cultural events are impossible to predict, Kurzweil believes that 'fundamental measures of information technology follow predictable and exponential trajectories, belying the conventional wisdom that 'you can't predict the future'.[15] Kurzweil used to subscribe to the logic of Moore's Law in his earlier predictions.[16] Moore's Law is derived from a comment made in 1965 by Gordon Moore, then CEO of Fairchild Semiconductor and later the co-founder of Intel, that the number of transistors on an integrated circuit board would double every year, while unit costs would fall correspondingly.[17] Moore subsequently revised this forecast to that number doubling every two years.[18] He then developed this observation into a theory of exponential growth, that Kurzweil himself applied not only to semi-conductor circuits but also other forms of technology.[19] The simple laptop, for example, has conformed broadly to these principles.

Exponential growth, however, cannot go on forever. As Murray Shanahan notes, the laws of physics dictate that every technological trend must meet a plateau eventually.[20] Rodney Brooks argues that the whole idea has been 'oversold'.[21] Meanwhile, Kurzweil himself came to believe that Moore's Law would not hold true beyond 2020. He has therefore developed his own 'Law of Accelerating Returns':

level of AI that will match human-level intelligence.[42] Not so long after this, according to Kurzweil, we will reach the Singularity. His most recent prediction for the date of the Singularity is 2045.[43]

The term, 'singularity' comes from physics, and refers to a moment, such as the Big Bang, when mathematics begins to break down, and so does our comprehension.[44] John von Neumann subsequently relates the term to the accelerating pace of technological development, which Stanislaw Ulam paraphrases as the moment when 'the ever accelerating progress of technology . . . gives the appearance of approaching some singularity in the history of the race beyond which human affairs, as we know them, could not continue'.[45] Vernon Vinge later further expanded this definition, coining the term the 'technological singularity':

> What are the consequences of this event? When greater-than-human intelligence drives progress, that progress will be much more rapid. In fact, there seems no reason why progress itself would not involve the creation of still more intelligent entities – on a still-shorter time scale. The best analogy that I see is with the evolutionary past: Animals can adapt to problems and make inventions, but often no faster than natural selection can do its work – the world acts as its own simulator. We humans have the ability to internalize the world and conduct 'what if's' in our heads; we can solve many problems thousands of times faster than natural selection. Now, by creating the means to execute those simulations at much higher speeds, we are entering a regime as radically different from our human past as we humans are from the lower animals. From the human point of view, this change will be a throwing away of all the previous rules, perhaps in a blink of an eye, an exponential runway beyond any hope of control.[46]

Kurzweil builds upon these earlier descriptions and describes the Singularity as an explosion of intelligence, a moment of technological change so rapid that it amounts to a 'rupture in the fabric of human history', with enormous consequences for the future of the human race:

> Within a few decades, machine intelligence will surpass human intelligence, leading to the Singularity – technological change so

rapid and profound it represents a rupture in the fabric of human history. The implications include the merger of biological and nonbiological intelligence, immortal software-based humans, and ultra-high levels of intelligence that expand outward in the universe at the speed of light.[47]

From a philosophical perspective, David Chalmers agrees with Kurzweil that the Singularity is indeed possible.[48] Meanwhile, although some are ambivalent – or even negative – about the impact of these developments, Kurzweil himself is unequivocally positive. Machines have already improved our lives, and Kurzweil believes that they are likely to improve them still further: 'What's actually happening is [machines] are powering all of us. They're making us smarter. They may not yet be inside our bodies, but, by the 2030s, we will connect our neocortex, the part of our brain where we do our thinking, to the cloud.'[49] Kurzweil is convinced that machines will not only make us more intelligent, but will also bring other benefits to humanity: 'We're going to be funnier, we're going to be better at music. We're going to be sexier.'[50]

AGI and beyond

Following the Singularity, the next stage would be for machines to achieve Strong AI or Artificial General Intelligence (AGI). To achieve AGI, it is not simply a question of a computer passing the Turing Test.[51] To pass the Turing Test, after all, a computer only needs to *appear* to be more than a chat bot trained to give automatic responses. Rather, to achieve AGI a computer must be *genuinely* capable of thinking for itself. This is not so straightforward.[52] To do so, it needs to be sentient and have consciousness.[53] Perhaps the biggest problem with AGI, however, is that as yet we still do not fully understand human consciousness. Until such time as we can actually understand consciousness, it is difficult to speculate when AGI might ever be achieved.

Clearly we are still a long way from reaching AGI. Nonetheless, most working in the field of AI believe that AGI is achievable. David Chalmers, one of the leading philosophers of consciousness, is certainly confident that it can be achieved.[54] He also believes that the development of GPT-3 by OpenAI has brought the possibility of AGI much closer.[55] Indeed, OpenAI, like other leading AI companies, such as DeepMind, is dedicated to developing AGI. Certainly, for Kurzweil, there is no question that – eventually – we will achieve AGI. His latest prediction for the advent of AGI is the year 2045.

Once AGI has been achieved, it is a relatively short step to superintelligence or artificial superintelligence (ASI). As soon as machines become capable of thinking for themselves, they would also be able to improve themselves, and their full potential would be unleashed. Superintelligence can take many forms.[56] Nick Bostrom defines it as 'any intellect that greatly exceeds the cognitive performance of humans in virtually all domains of interest'.[57] The possibilities of ASI are seemingly endless:

> By definition, an ASI can perform better than us in any conceivable task, including intellectual skills. It could engage in scientific research and teach itself new abilities, improve its own code, create unlimited copies of itself, choose better ways of deploying its computational resources, and it could even transform the environment on Earth, or colonise other planets.[58]

Closely aligned with superintelligence is the notion of 'ultraintelligence', a term that Good coined back in 1965:

> A machine that can far surpass all intellectual activities of any man however clever. Since the design of machines is one of these intellectual activities, an ultraintelligent machine could design even better machines. There would then unquestionably be an 'intelligence explosion,' and the intelligence of man would be left far behind. Thus the first ultraintelligent machine is the last invention that man need ever make.[59]

The question remains, of course, as to whether we would even be able to recognise the intelligence of a superintelligent or ultraintelligent machine, in that the intelligence that it would display would be far beyond our comprehension. As Elon Musk comments, 'The biggest mistake that I see artificial intelligence researchers making is assuming that they're intelligent. Yeah, they're not, compared to AI.

And so like, a lot of them cannot imagine something smarter than themselves, but AI will be vastly smarter – vastly.'[60]

The biggest issue, however, is that the ultraintelligent or superintelligent machine would effectively be the last invention that human kind would ever need to make, in that once we reach that point, superintelligent machines would be able to design even more intelligent machines, and human beings would never be able to compete. Game over.

Prediction errors

'Prediction is very difficult,' Niels Bohr remarks, 'especially about the future.'[61] Get it right, and everyone will tell you that it was obvious that it would happen. Get it wrong, and everyone will tell you that it was equally obvious that it would never happen. Predictions also tend to be strewn with errors.[62] This is why techniques such as backpropagation are used to correct errors and improve the accuracy of predictions in AI. But predictions about the future of AI itself seem to be particularly problematic.

Dates themselves are difficult enough. Take predictions about 'human-level intelligence'. Turing predicted that we would reach this stage by 2000, while Kurzweil predicts that we will reach it by 2029.[63] Martin Ford conducted a survey, with the median date being 2099.[64] But in fact there have been many different surveys of timelines, none of which agree.[65]

Or take predictions about the Singularity. Kurzweil predicts that it will happen by 2045. But in the catalogue for the recent *AI: More than Human* exhibition at the Barbican in London, AI specialists Kanta Dihal, Andrew Hessel, Amy Robinson Sterling and Francesca Rossi were invited to predict the date of the Singularity, and, significantly, none of them could agree on the date.[66]

Or take predictions about AGI. Although Kurzweil expects AGI to be achieved by 2045, Rodney Brooks thinks that we still have a long way to go, and does not expect that we will see AGI until 2200: 'Any AI program in the world right now is an idiot savant living in the sea of now.'[67]

The real problem, however, is that there is even less agreement about the actual definition of these terms. Rossi conflates the

Singularity with AGI.[68] Likewise, Ford conflates 'human level AI' with AGI.[69] Meanwhile Russell considers that the quest for AGI is really just the quest for AI itself: 'AGI is actually what we have always called artificial intelligence. We are just not finished yet, and we have not created AGI yet.'[70]

By contrast, Kevin Kelly believes that the entire project of AGI is misconceived.[71] Hassabis even argues that intelligence and consciousness do not even depend upon each other: 'You can have intelligence without consciousness, and you can have consciousness without human-level intelligence.'[72] Roger Penrose concurs with this view.[73] Seth also agrees: 'Consciousness and intelligence are entirely different things. You don't have to be smart to suffer, but you probably have to be alive.'[74] Meanwhile, as Kurzweil observes, a machine might act as though it has a mind, regardless of whether it has a mind or not.[75] This is borne out by the development of GPT-3 by OpenAI, which is quite capable of claiming that it is sentient, when asked, even though it is clearly not.[76] This is not to say that GPT-3 is actually 'lying'. In fact it is not aware of anything, still less whether it is lying or not. It is simply selecting the most appropriate answer from the vast dataset of human operations on which it has been trained.[77] Revealingly, however, this also suggests that human beings themselves are perhaps not as honest as they like to think they are.

Consciousness, as Max Tegmark remarks, is probably all that humans beings will be able to cling on to, once computers exceed the intellect of human beings: 'We humans have built out identity of being *Homo sapiens*, the smartest entities around. As we prepare to be humbled by ever smarter machines, I suggest that we rebrand ourselves as *Homo sentiens*!'[78] Besides, if we see the world in terms of extended intelligence, as a coupling between human and machine, the need for a machine to also have consciousness seems less imperative. Indeed, as Musk observes, thanks to the prosthetic logic of extended intelligence, humans are already superhumans.[79]

In short, the Singularity and AGI remain difficult to define, let alone to predict.[80] There is little consensus as to what they might be, still less as to when they might happen. The same could be said of superintelligence. Despite Kurzweil's optimism, it seems that superintelligence is also still a long way off. As Rodney Brooks observes, 'We don't have anything near as good as an insect, so I'm not afraid of superintelligence showing up any time soon.'[81] In some senses, however, these questions are purely academic, or as Brooks puts it, 'Predicting an AI future is just a power game for isolated academics who live in a bubble away from the real world.'[82]

The future of intelligence

How will AI be perceived once it has been completely integrated into our lives?

Back in 2002, Bill Gates predicted that the first decade of the third millennium would be known as 'The Digital Decade' in that, by the time that it would come to an end, 'the impact of the digital realm would be so far-reaching that there would scarcely be any facet of human existence that would remain untouched by it.'[83] His prediction has proved largely accurate.[84]

Similarly, back in 2010 it was also predicted that by 2020 we would stop using the term 'digital' in architectural design circles.[85] This would not be because we would no longer be using digital design tools, but for precisely the opposite reason – almost everyone would be using digital tools. For this very reason, the term itself would disappear. The digital would be everywhere and nowhere.[86] We would therefore stop referring to 'digital design'. This prediction has also proved largely accurate. In many aspects, 'digital design' has become simply 'design'.

This is echoed in the way that we refer to drawings. Initially, when most drawings were drawn by hand, they were referred to as 'drawings', and CAD drawings were called 'digital drawings'. Once most drawings became CAD drawings, the term 'drawing' came to refer to CAD drawings, while the term 'hand drawings' came to refer to drawings drawn by hand. In other words, now that the tipping point has been reached when more drawings are produced computationally than drawn by hand, CAD drawings have become simply 'drawings'.

A similar analogy could be made in relation to cars. In the very early days, when there were relatively few cars on the road, they were referred to as 'horseless carriages', and carriages drawn by horses were still referred to as 'carriages'. However, once 'horseless carriages' came to outnumber 'carriages', then the situation changed, and 'horseless carriages' became known as 'cars', and carriages drawn by horses became known as a 'horse-drawn carriages'. By extension, we could predict that once self-driving cars outnumber cars driven by humans, self-driving cars will become known simply as 'cars' and what we now call 'cars' will become known as 'human-driven cars'. And what about AI? Are we now in 'The AI Decade'? And what might we predict about the way we will refer to AI by the end of this decade? At present, we distinguish between AI and human intelligence, and refer to human intelligence simply as 'intelligence'. With time, however, as AI becomes increasingly prevalent and more powerful than human intelligence, we are likely to reach another tipping point. Could we predict that by the end of the decade, AI will simply be known as 'intelligence', and what we now call 'intelligence' will become known as 'human intelligence'? And might we even begin to view 'human intelligence' with a degree of sentimentality, just as we now view horse-drawn carriages, handwritten letters and hand-drawn drawings?

'The quest for AI is the quest for intelligence itself.'

The irony of AI being called 'intelligence' is that when John McCarthy originally coined the term 'artificial intelligence' back in 1956, he and others did not really it, but, as McCarthy points out, 'I had to call it something, so I called it "Artificial Intelligence".'[87] His goal, however, was to achieve *genuine* – rather than artificial – intelligence. This is still the case with many contemporary AI researchers. Besides, as Walsh observes, 'Putting the adjective *artificial* in front of anything never sounds very good.'[88] Stibel also claims that the word 'artificial' is misleading, causing people to associate AI with something fake or 'less than' intelligent. Instead, Stibel notes, what is needed is an artificial brain to create real intelligence, 'much in the way that an artificial heart is used to create a real heartbeat'.[89]

Interestingly, many of the central figures in AI have been more concerned about understanding how the brain works. Turing, as we have already seen, had confessed that he was more interested in how the brain works than in the practical applications of computing.[90] Likewise, Geoffrey Hinton, now a luminary within the world of AI, initially studied physiology for a particular reason: 'I wanted to know how the brain worked.'[91] Demis Hassabis, who holds a PhD in neuroscience and is CEO of DeepMind, does not refer to AI but simply to 'intelligent systems': 'Our ambition in DeepMind is to build intelligent systems to help find solutions that can learn to solve any complex problem . . . Put another way, we want to use it to solve everything else.'[92]

The quest for AI is the quest for intelligence itself.

Architectural intelligence

The applications of AI and data-driven informational systems have now become so widespread throughout the domain of architecture that we should perhaps refer to them collectively as contributing to a form of 'architectural intelligence', an intelligent approach to architectural design that is fast becoming the dominant approach.[93]

Makoto sei Watanabe is probably the first to use the term 'architectural intelligence' to refer to a new type of architectural designer, the 'AI Tect', exploring the potential of AI in architecture.[94] Wanyu He has also coined a similar term, the 'AI-chitect', to refer to a

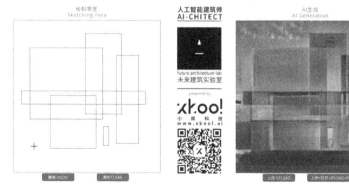

FIGURE 8.3 Xkool, AI-chitect, *Eyes of the City*, Bi-City Biennale of Urbanism and Architecture, Hong Kong-Shenzhen, 2019. AI-chitect is a neural network trained to translate schematic sketches into architectural drawings, similar to how Nvidia's GauGAN translates sketches into painting-like representations.

very similar kind of designer.[95] Let us not forget, of course, that Molly Wright Steenson also uses the term in a more narrow sense, to refer to four pioneers in the field of computational architecture.[96]

In this context, however, 'architectural intelligence' is not limited to the application of AI. It could be used to refer to a new approach to design that embraces *all* forms of intelligence in architecture, such as 'structural intelligence', 'environmental intelligence', 'constructional intelligence', 'programmatic intelligence' and so on. It is a new approach that has already been defined: 'A new movement is emerging. It is a movement that operates at the interface between advanced digital technologies and the built environment . . . We are calling this new movement "*architectural intelligence*".'[97]

Nor is architectural intelligence limited to the digital. We can find examples of 'biological intelligence' throughout nature. Indeed nature itself offers countless examples that can inspire a biological approach towards design. This informs the work of architects such as Achim Menges, Neri Oxman and Claudia Pasquero, who draw upon biomimicry and biomimetic principles. So too, we can find examples of 'material intelligence' throughout the natural kingdom. This could even be described as a form of 'material computation'. The form of a sand dune, for example, is 'computed' through the force of wind and gravity on the particles of sand. Likewise, the form of a soap bubble is 'computed' through a combination of forces, such as internal and external pressure, surface tension and so on. This, in turn, informs the work of architects such as Antoni Gaudí and Frei Otto, who draw upon material behaviours and morphogenetic principles.[98]

Buildings, of course, are material, whereas computation is immaterial. However, we can now use intelligent computational techniques, such as AI, to inform the intelligent design of a material building and make our designs ever more materially intelligent. Architectural intelligence therefore stands not only for the intelligent use of materials and the use of 'intelligent materials' in the construction of a building, but also for the use of intelligent computational techniques to design the material form of that building.

How might we refer to 'architectural intelligence' in the future, once the various forms of intelligence – structural intelligence, environmental intelligence, material intelligence, programmatic intelligence and so on – have become increasingly prevalent in architectural circles? Could we predict, perhaps, that once every aspect of design has become intelligent, the term 'intelligence' would cancel itself out? Would references to 'intelligence' disappear? If so, all that we would be left with would simply be 'architecture'.

AI and the future of architecture

Undoubtedly, however, there will be some opposition to the introduction of AI into the architectural studio, just as there was opposition to the introduction of computation. We could predict that AI might also be banned from some architectural studios, just as computers were once banned in certain schools of architecture.[99] But this opposition is likely to fade away eventually, as happened with the initial opposition to computation itself.[100] Indeed, some might choose not to use AI, even though it will obviously prove more convenient, just as some hipsters today deliberately choose to ride bicycles instead of driving cars, as a lifestyle choice.[101] Clearly, AI will not be for everyone.

It is the example of the self-driving car, however, that might shed some light on the full implications of introducing AI into architecture. Christensen, as we have noted, compares the introduction of AI into the architectural office with the development of the self-driving car.[102] There is, however, a problem with this analogy.

AI, of course, will make life easier, just like self-driving cars. With self-driving cars, however, the driver eventually becomes redundant. If we adopt the same model for architecture, would this not mean that eventually the architect would also become redundant?[103] Rather than striving for the equivalent of the self-driving car in architecture, should we perhaps keep to the model that Wolf Prix suggests, with the architects in the front seats, and AI in the back seats?

Or is it already too late to prevent these developments? Might the architect also disappear, just as the human driver will disappear? And might we not notice or even care?

Let us finish, then, with a series of predictions about the future impact of AI on architecture, based on comments made above. These are predictions as to what will be technically possible – although not perhaps implemented universally – by the end of the decade:

1   AI will become part of the curriculum in every school of architecture.

2   Architecture will become intelligent.

3   Cities will be controlled by AI.[104]

4   Facial recognition will mean that we no longer need passports, keys, credit cards or cash.[105]

5   We will communicate with our computers through speech and hand gestures. Writing and drawing skills will begin to fade.[106]

6   AI will become an indispensible, invisible assistant in all architectural offices, automating the design process.[107]

7   Initial resistance to AI will begin to fade, as AI becomes unavoidable.[108]

8   Clients will insist on their architects using AI.[109]

9   Architects will brand themselves in terms of their use of AI.[110]

10 AI will be able to generate customised designs, completely autonomously.[111]

Welcome to architecture in the age of AI!

Notes

Acknowledgements

1 Leon Battista Alberti, *On the Art of Building in Ten Books*, Joseph Rykwert, Neil Leach and Robert Tavernor (trans.), Cambridge, MA: MIT Press, 1988.

Preface

1 Turing quoted in *The Times* newspaper in 1949. Turing is here referring to an early computer called the 'mechanical mind', rather than to AI as such. Dermot Turing, *Prof: Alan Turing Decoded*, Norwich: Pitkin Publishing, 2015, https://quoteinvestigator.com/2019/10/12/ai-shadow.

2 Quoted in R. Cellan-Jones, 'Stephen Hawking Warns Artificial Intelligence Could End Mankind,' *BBC News*, 2 December 2014, https://www.bbc.com/news/technology-30290540.

3 M. McFarland, 'Elon Musk: "With Artificial Intelligence, We Are Summoning the Demon"', *Washington Post*, 24 October 2014, https://www.washingtonpost.com/news/innovations/wp/2014/10/24/elon-musk-with-artificial-intelligence-we-are-summoning-the-demon/.

4 Stuart Russell and Peter Norvig, *Artificial Intelligence: A Modern Approach*, New York: Pearson Inc, 2010; Stop Autonomous Weapons, *Slaughterbots*, https://www.youtube.com/watch?v=9CO6M2HsoIA.

Introduction

1 At the time of writing, when asked the question, 'Alexa, are you artificial intelligence?', Alexa replies, 'I like to imagine myself a bit like an Aurora Borealis, a surge of charged multi-coloured photons dancing through the atmosphere.'

2   https://nest.com; Anne-Sophie Garrigou, 'So what does a smart city really look like?', *The Beam*, 23 July 2018.

3   Rodney Brooks, CEO of iRobot, a company that produces automatic, self-directed robotic floor cleaners, predicts that robots will soon take on other responsibilities within the home, such as cleaning toilets. Brian Bergstein, 'A Top Roboticist Says A.I. Will Not Conquer Humanity', *Medium Future*, 4 January 2019, https://medium.com/s/2069/a-top-roboticist-says-a-i-will-not-conquer-humanity-133f2611d035.

4   https://www.parking-net.com/parking-news/pixevia/artificial-intelligence-smart-parking.

5   For a comparison between AI and the replicants in *Blade Runner*, see Neil Leach, 'Do Robots Dream of Digital Sheep?', in Kory Bieg, Danelle Briscoe and Clay Odom (eds), *ACADIA 2019: Ubiquity and Autonomy, Proceedings of the 39th Annual Conference of the Association for Computer Aided Design in Architecture*, University of Texas at Austin, Texas, 2019, pp. 298–309.

6   Schools that already use AI in the design studio include the Architectural Association (AA), Bartlett School of Architecture, University College London (Bartlett), Carnegie Mellon University (CMU), Florida Atlantic University (FAU), Florida International University (FIU), Harvard Graduate School of Design (GSD), University of Innsbruck (Innsbruck), Massachusetts Institute of Technology (MIT), University of California Los Angeles (UCLA), University of Michigan (Michigan), Southern California Institute of Architecture (SCI-Arc) and Tongji University (Tongji).

7   Lectures about AI frequently attract several thousand views. For DigitalFUTURES lectures on AI: https://www.youtube.com/watch?v=2YO0loKIzBg&list=PLtuu5idZ57EWto42aIJP-XImsRf9jmWoR For FIU DDes lectures on AI: https://www.youtube.com/watch?v=6U-0_VgD9s8&list=PLjgJTkiYXdLfjR2Lf31_A9huoSPVWomhm.

8   The DigitalFUTURES initiative has run numerous workshops on AI: https://www.digitalfutures.world.

9   At the 2019 conference for the Association for Advanced Computer Aided Design in Architecture (ACADIA) in Austin, Texas, two full sessions were dedicated to AI.

10 A number of AI-based doctoral research projects have been undertaken within MIT Media Lab. One of the most interesting is Street Score, a machine learning algorithm that predicts the perceived safety of a street: https://www.media.mit.edu/projects/streetscore/overview/.

11 MIT now runs an undergraduate programme in Urban Science and Planning with Computer Science that brings together AI and

urbanism: http://urban-science.mit.edu/. New York University in Shanghai (NYU Shanghai) runs a masters programme in AI and Culture. Some programmes, such as the DDes programme at FIU, have a particular focus on the theory of AI, and AI-based architectural design.

12 Spacemaker AI was acquired by Autodesk in November 2020.

13 James Bridle, *New Dark Age: Technology and the End of the Future*, London: Verso, 2018; Shoshana Zuboff, *The Age of Surveillance Capitalism*, New York: Hachette, 2018.

14 Instead, perhaps, we need to engage with the rapidly developing world of cognitive science, when dealing with AI. Cognitive science is an umbrella term embracing a series of related disciplines, including AI, neuroscience and philosophy.

15 Heidegger was once popular among architects, and it was his thinking that helped to fuel the denigration of computation in the early days of Computer Aided Design (CAD). At the University of Cambridge in the 1990s, where theoretical debates were dominated by reference to Heidegger and other similar thinkers, computers were banned from the architectural studio. Heidegger is still celebrated by the Object Oriented Ontology (OOO) movement, typified by Graham Harman. In his famous analysis of tools, for example, Heidegger argues that either we are familiar with a tool, and know how to use it, or unfamiliar, and have no sense of how to use it. Harman's continued celebration of Heidegger's understanding of tools now seems somewhat dated: Graham Harman, *Tool-Being: Heidegger and the Metaphysics of Objects*, Chicago: Open Court, 2002. See Jonathan Hale, 'Harman on Heidegger: "Buildings as Tool-Beings"', *Body of Theory*, 29 May 2013, https://bodyoftheory.com/2013/05/29/. For a critique of Harman and Heidegger, see Neil Leach, 'Digital Tool Thinking: Object Oriented Ontology versus New Materialism', in Kathy Velikov, Sean Ahlquist, Matias del Campo and Geoffrey Thün (eds), *ACADIA 2016: Posthuman Frontiers: Data, Designers and Cognitive Machines, Proceedings of the 36th Annual Conference of the Association for Computer Aided Design in Architecture*, n.p.p.: n.p., 2016, pp. 344 51.

16 See Hale, 'Harman on Heidegger'.

17 Roland Barthes, 'The Eiffel Tower', in Neil Leach (ed.), *Rethinking Architecture: A Reader in Cultural Theory*, London: Routledge, 1997, p. 164.

18 See Leach, 'Digital Tool Thinking', pp. 344–51.

19 See Neil Leach, 'Forget Heidegger', in Neil Leach (ed.), *Designing for a Digital World*, London: Wiley, 2002, pp. 21–30; Neil Leach, *Forget Heidegger*, Bucharest: Paideia, 2006.

20 Maurice Merleau-Ponty, *Phenomenology of Perception*, London: Routledge, 2012, p. 153

21 Jonathan Hale, 'Materiality, Movement and Meaning: Architecture and the Embodied Mind', keynote lecture, *Proceedings of the Annual Architectural Research Symposium in Finland*, 2014, 305–14, https://journal.fi/atut/article/view/48277.

22 See Neil Leach, *Camouflage*, Cambridge, MA: MIT Press, 2006.

23 Andy Clark and David J. Chalmers, 'The Extended Mind', *Analysis* 58 (1998): 7–19.

24 This issue is often referred to as the mind/body problem.

25 N. Katherine Hayles, *How We Became Post-Human*, Chicago: University of Chicago Press, 1999.

26 Manfred Clynes and Nathan Kline, 'Cyborgs and Space', *Astronautics* (September 1960): 26–76, reprinted in, C. Gray (ed.), *The Cyborg Handbook*, London: Routledge, 1995, pp. 29–34.

27 Donna Haraway, 'A Cyborg Manifesto: Science, Technology, and Socialist-Feminism in the Late Twentieth Century', in *Simians, Cyborgs and Women: The Reinvention of Nature*. New York: Routledge, 1991.

28 D. Haraway, 'Cyborgs and symbionts: living together in the new world order', in C. Gray (ed.), *The Cyborg Handbook*, London: Routledge, 1995, p. xix.

29 Haraway, 'A Cyborg Manifesto'.

30 Jonathan Hale describes how a blind person can become one with his/her white cane. Jonathan Hale, 'Materiality, Movement and Meaning'.

31 The theory of affordances was introduced initially by James Gibson in an article: James Gibson, 'The Theory of Affordances', in Robert Shaw and John Bransford (eds), *Perceiving, Acting, and Knowing*, London: Wiley, 1977. Gibson later elaborated on this theory in his book: James Gibson, *The Ecological Approach to Visual Perception*, Hove: Psychology Press, 1979. It was also developed by Gibson's wife, Eleanor Gibson together with Anne Pick: Eleanor Gibson and Anne Pick, *An Ecological Approach to Perceptual Learning and Development*, New York: Oxford University Press, 2000. As I have noted elsewhere, 'The theory of affordances suggests that there is a particular action or set of actions that is afforded by a tool or object. Thus a knob might afford pulling – or possibly pushing – while a cord might afford pulling. This is not to say that the tool or object has agency as such. In other words the tool or object does not have the capacity to actually "invite" or "prevent" certain actions. Rather it simply "affords" certain operations that it is incumbent on the user to recognise, dependent in part on a set of pre-existing associations that have been made with that tool or object. Likewise that action or set of actions is also dependent upon the capacity of an individual to undertake those actions. Thus certain actions might not be afforded to small children or those without the strength or agility to perform those actions. Moreover, certain tools afford certain operations, but do not preclude other operations. For example, we might perhaps affix a nail with a screwdriver – albeit less efficiently – if we do not have a hammer at hand. We might also recognize that it is easier to cut wood with a saw than with a hammer, and that the technique of cutting with a saw affords a limited range of possible operations. Importantly also the theory of affordances has been applied to human computer interfaces to refer to the easy discoverability of certain actions. As such, we might be able to identify various operations afforded by digital tools that might thereby become popular.' Neil Leach, 'There is No Such Thing as Parametric Architecture; There is No Such Thing as Political Architecture', in Matthew Poole and Manuel Shvartzberg (eds), *The Politics of Parametricism*, London: Bloomsbury, 2015, pp. 58–78.

32 Here I would challenge in the strongest possible terms the notion that Bruno Latour has advanced in his Actor Network Theory (ANT) that tools 'act' in social networks. Bruno Latour [Jim Johnson], 'Mixing Humans with Non-Humans: Sociology of a Door-Closer, *Social Problems* 35, no. 3 (1988): 298–310. For my critique of this notion, see Leach, 'Digital Tool Thinking', pp. 344–51.

33 'Elon's Message on Artificial Superintelligence – ASI', *Science Time*, 24 October 2020, https://www.youtube.com/watch?v=ZCeOsdcQO bl&feature=youtu.be. See also Amber Case, 'We Are All Cyborgs Now', *TEDWomen*, 2010, https://www.ted.com/talks/amber_case_ we_are_all_cyborgs_now?language=en.

34 Good design facilitates this process of assimilation: Leach, *Camouflage*.

35 'Elon's Message on Artificial Superintelligence – ASI'.

36 Andy Clark, *Natural Born Cyborgs: Minds, Technologies, and the Future of Human Intelligence*. Oxford: Oxford University Press, 2003.

37 E. Bennett, M. Diamond, D. Krech et al., 'Chemical and Anatomical Plasticity of the Brain', *Science*. 146, no. 3644 (1964): 610–19.

38 Clark, *Natural Born Cyborgs*, p. 31.

39 Clark, *Natural Born Cyborgs*, p. 142.

40 Joichi Ito, 'Resisting Reduction: A Manifesto', *Journal of Design and Science: MIT Media Lab*, 1 November 2017, https://jods.mitpress. mit.edu/pub/ resisting-reduction.

41 Anant Jhingran, 'Obsessing about AI is the Wrong Way to Think about the Future', *Wired*, 22 January 2016, https://www. wired.

12 This, at least, is the view taken by Alan Turing, who takes the position that in order to think, one must first be able to feel. Alan Turing, 'Computing Machinery and Intelligence,' *Mind* 59, no. 236, (1950): 433–60. As such, we need to question the title of Toby Walsh's recent book. Toby Walsh, *Machines that Think: The Future of Artificial Intelligence*, New York: Prometheus Books, 2018.

13 Russell in Ford, *Architects of Intelligence*, p. 40.

14 Pedro Domingos, *The Master Algorithm: Why the Quest for the Ultimate Learning Machine will Remake the World*, New York: Basic Books, 2018, p. 8.

15 Mitchell, *Artificial Intelligence*, p. 21.

16 Kelleher, *Deep Learning*, p. 252.

17 Alan Clements, *Principles of Computer Hardware*, Oxford: Oxford University Press, 1985.

18 According to Stanford's AI index report of 2017, 'there has been a 14 fold increase in the number of active AI startups since 2000'. Louis Columbus, '10 Charts That Will Change Your Perspective On Artificial Intelligence's Growth', *Forbes*, 12 January 2018, https://www.forbes.com/sites/louiscolumbus/2018/01/12/10-charts-that-will-change-your-perspective-on-artificial-intelligences-growth/#79ea4c284758.

19 It has been claimed that data doubles every eighteen months. 'Humanity Doubles its Data Collection Every 18 Months, and It Has Powerful Implications', *Flux*, https://www.fluxmagazine.com/data-creation-powerful-implications/.

20 Boden, *AI*, p. 47.

21 Kelleher, *Deep Learning*, p. 255.

22 Supervised learning and reinforcement learning, however, also play a role in learning a language.

23 This might be compared to the role of mimesis: 'We may see [mimesis] at work also when a child learns to speak and adapt to the world. In fact, it is precisely the example of the child "growing into" language that best illustrates the operation of mimesis. The child "absorbs" an external language by a process of imitation, then uses it creatively for its own purposes. Similarly, within the realm of architecture we might see mimesis at work as architects develop their design abilities: it is this process which also allows external forms to be absorbed and sedimented, and then rearticulated as an individual expression.' Leach, *Camouflage*, pp. 21–2.

24 Merrit Kennedy, 'Computer Learns To Play Go At Superhuman Levels "Without Human Knowledge"', *NPR*, 18 October 2017, https://www.npr.org/sections/thetwo-way/2017/10/18/558519095/

computer-learns-to-play-go-at-superhuman-levels-without-human-knowledge.

25 Domingos, *The Master Algorithm*.

26 'Evolutionaries believe that the mother of all learning is natural selection. If it made us, it can make everything, and all we need to do is simulate it on the computer.' Domingos, *The Master Algorithm*, p. 52.

27 'Bayesians are concerned above all with uncertainty. All learned knowledge is uncertain, and learning itself is a form of uncertain inference.' Domingos, *The Master Algorithm*, p. 52.

28 'For analogizers, the key to learning is recognising similarities between different situations and thereby inferring other similarities. If two patients have similar symptoms, perhaps they have the same disease. The key problem is judging how similar two things are.' Domingos, *The Master Algorithm*, p. 53.

29 Domingos, *The Master Algorithm*, p. 52.

30 For backpropagation see p. 23.

31 Domingos, *The Master Algorithm*, p. 52.

32 This will be discussed in greater detail in the next chapter.

33 These terms are, of course, borrowed from neuroscience. It is important to recognise, however, that they refer to purely mathematical models and not biological mechanisms.

34 Ethem Alpaydin, *Machine Learning*, Cambridge, MA: MIT Press, 2016, p. 178.

35 Boden, *AI*, p. 79.

36 Boden, *AI*, p. 79.

37 Although the features themselves do not need to be handcrafted, the network architecture itself still needs to be handcrafted, so that it becomes task specific.

38 As Memo Akten notes, 'The deep learning model is essentially a stack of parameterised, non-linear feature transformations that can be used to learn hierarchical representations.' Memo Akten, 'Background info for "#Deepdream is blowing my mind"', *Medium*, 9 July 2015, https://medium.com/@memoakten/background-info-for-deepdream-is-blowing-my-mind-1983fb7420d9.

39 Another important distinction is that the networks in the human brain are dynamic, which means that there is a temporal component to how information is encoded and processed, whereas with deep learning neural networks, and specifically convolutional neural networks, there is no temporal component.

40 Yoshua Bengio interviewed by Martin Ford, in Ford, *Architects of Intelligence*, p. 23.

41 Mitchell, *Artificial Intelligence*, p. 37. The term 'digit' here refers to 'visual feature' or 'data feature'.

42 Russell in Ford, *Architects of Intelligence*, p. 42.

43 The significant breakthrough in the domain of image classification came when Fei-Fei Li, a young researcher at Princeton, realised that it would be possible to use the principles adopted in the lexical database WordNet to create ImageNet, an image-based processing system. Whereas WordNet was based on nouns, ImageNet exploited the system by linking nouns to images that contained examples of those nouns. The system depended, however, on vast resources of human labour to label images, deploying Amazon's Mechanical Turk, often referred to as 'artificial artificial intelligence'. Mitchell, *Artificial Intelligence*, pp. 82–90.

44 A convolution could be described conceptually as a 2D filter that loops over windows of pixels, looking for specific visual features. Each neuron in a convolutional layer will learn to extract (or activate to) a different 2D visual feature, such as an edge or a curve.

45 Anil K. Seth, 'A predictive processing theory of sensorimotor contingencies: Explaining the puzzle of perceptual presence and its absence in synesthesia', *Cognitive neuroscience* 5, no. 2 (2014): 97–118, doi:10.1080/17588928.2013.877880; Andy Clark, *Surfing Uncertainty: Prediction, Action and the Embodied Mind*, Oxford: Oxford University Press, 2016.

46 The reason why they are described as 'maps' is that they operate in 2D, as opposed to neural networks which operate based on one-dimensional inputs. For further details on ConvNets, see I. Goodfellow, Y. Bengio and A. Courville, *Deep Learning*, Cambridge, MA: MIT Press, 2016.

47 Foster describes generative modelling as follows: 'A generative model describes how a dataset is generated, in terms of a probabilistic model. By sampling from this model, we are able to generate new data.' Foster, *Generative Deep Learning*, p. 1.

48 DeepDream was developed initially as a technique to visualise features that a neuron or layer would activate or learn to extract from its input. The programme was based on earlier research undertaken by others as part of the ImageNet Large-Scale Visual Recognition Challenge (ILSVRC) in 2014. Christian Szegedy, Wei Lu, Yangqing Jia, Pierre Sermanet, Scott Reed, Dragomir Anguelov, Dumitru Erhan, Vincent Vanhoucke and Andrew Rabinovich, 'Going Deeper with Convolutions', *Computing Research Repository* (2014), https://arxiv.org/abs/1409.4842

49 The practice of generating an image, however, is more usually done using visual saliency mapping, a procedure not dissimilar to DeepDream, but one which does not involve multiple iterations of pixel manipulations.

50 To be precise, it can only generate an image of the features that a neural network has learnt to associate with the category 'cat' from its training dataset. It is not mathematically possible for DeepDream to reproduce an actual image of a cat, as there are many different kinds of images that could satisfy the requirements for the cat category. DeepDream cannot project from the category label to one of those specific images because there is insufficient information provided. However, if it is given an input image, it can emphasise the features associated with the cat class, which results in a trippy, pareidolia-like image.

51 Akten, 'Background info for '#Deepdream is blowing my mind'. As Memo Akten comments (somewhat tongue-in-cheek), 'A very crude way of putting this is you give the network a completely random picture that looks nothing like a cat and you ask it '*does this look like a cat?*', the network says '*no*'. You make a few random changes and ask '*what about this?*', and the network says '*no*'. And you keep repeating. If the network says '*yea, maybe that looks a bit more like a cat*' you say '*aha! ok so I'll make more changes in that direction, how about this?*'. It's actually not exactly like that, but you get the idea. And you can see why it takes so long.' https://medium.com/@memoakten/background-info-for-deepdream-is-blowing-my-mind-1983fb7420d9.

52 The challenge of inverting the operation of a neural net in order to generate images is not so straightforward. The process cannot literally be inverted, as it is a non-linear operation, and therefore some ingenuity is required. As Blaise Aguera y Arcas explains, 'With a convolutional net you can't do this directly exactly, as it is not a linear operator, and therefore not invertible. But you can "cheat", by basically saying that I am going to optimize the pixels, so I'll start maybe with noise – with pure noise – and run the same gradient ascent algorithms that you use to learn a neural net on the pixels until the output corresponds to the embedding vector that I want.' Blaise Aguera y Arcas, 'How Computers are Learning to be Creative', TED Talk, 2016, https://www.ted.com/talks/blaise_aguera_y_arcas_how_computers_are_learning_to_be_creative?language=en.

53 'The problem,' as Aguera y Arcas notes, 'is that the convolutional nets are designed to be invariant to pose, which means that when they are run backwards they do not know what pose to render things in. This leads to an aggregation of several poses at once.'

64 Tero Karras, Samuli Laine and Timo Aila, 'A Style Based Generator Architecture for Generative Adversarial Networks', 12 December 2018, https://arxiv.org/pdf/1812.04948.pdf.

65 There is even a website that automatically generates highly realistic novel faces: https://www.thispersondoesnotexist.com/.

66 As the authors note, 'The new architecture leads to an automatically learned, unsupervised separation of high-level attributes (e.g., pose and identity when trained on human faces) and stochastic variation in the generated images (e.g., freckles, hair), and it enables intuitive, scale-specific control of the synthesis.' Karras, Laine and Aila, 'A Style Based Generator Architecture'.

67 Prince Grover comments that 'All the algorithms in machine learning rely on minimizing or maximizing a function, which we call "objective function". The group of functions that are minimized are called "loss functions". A loss function is a measure of how good a prediction model does in terms of being able to predict the expected outcome. A most commonly used method of finding the minimum point of function is "gradient descent". Think of loss function like undulating mountain and gradient descent is like sliding down the mountain to reach the bottommost point.' Prince Grover, '5 Regression Loss Functions All Machine Learners Should Know', *Heartbeat*, 5 June 2018, https://heartbeat.fritz.ai/5-regression-loss-functions-all-machine-learners-should-know-4fb140e9d4b0.

68 Phillip Isola, Jun-Yan Zhu, Tinghui Zhou and Alexei A. Efros, 'Image-to-Image Translation with Conditional Adversarial Networks', 26 November 2018, https://arxiv.org/pdf/1611.07004.pdf.

69 Domain transfer should be understood here as the transfer of the appearance of one dataset on to another. Each dataset can be referred to as a domain that captures a specific subset of the visual world.

70 Jun-Yan Zhu, Taesung Park, Phillip Isola and Alexei Efros, 'Unpaired Image-to-Image Translation using Cycle-Consistent Adversarial Networks', in IEEE International Conference on Computer Vision (ICCV), 2017.

71 See, however, Yanghao Li, Naiyan Wang, Jiaying Liu and Xiaodi Hou, 'Demistifying Neural Style Transfer', https://arxiv.org/abs/1701.01036.

72 Mode collapse occurs when the generator learns to generate only one plausible output that the discriminator thinks is 'real', and it will not generate a wide variety of output images. As a result, it captures only one mode of visual information in the training data. The discriminator will eventually learn to always reject this output, but then the generator will slightly modify its output to beat the discriminator, causing the network to become trapped and never learn anything new.

73 Instead CycleGAN will learn translations from dataset A to dataset B, but it will have to prove that it is able to reconstruct the translation from dataset B to dataset A.

74 Ahmed Elgammal, Bingchen Liu, Mohamed Elhoseiny and Marian Mazzone, 'CAN: Creative Adversarial Networks, Generating "Art" by Learning About Styles and Deviating from Style Norms', 23 June 2017, https://arxiv.org/abs/1706.07068.

75 Elgammal et al., 'CAN'.

76 Elgammal et al., 'CAN'.

77 Tao Xu, Pengchuan Zhang, Qiuyuan Huang, Han Zhang, Zhe Gan, Xioalei Huang and Xiaodong He, 'AttnGAN: Fine-Grained Text to Image Generation with Attentional Generative Adversarial Networks', *Computer Science*, 28 November 2017, https://arxiv.org/abs/1711.10485.

78 'DALL-E: Creating Images from Text', *OpenAI Blog*, 5 January 2021, https://openai.com/blog/dall-e/.

79 Nikhila Ravi, Georgia Gkioxari and Justin Johnson, 'Introducing PyTorch3D: An open-source library for 3D deep learning', *Facebook AI*, 6 February 2020, https://ai.facebook.com/blog/-introducing-pytorch3d-an-open-source-library-for-3d-deep-learning/.

80 Nikhila Ravi explains: 'One of the reasons 3D understanding with deep learning is relatively underexplored compared with 2D understanding is because 3D data inputs are more complex with more memory and computation requirements, whereas 2D images can be represented by simple tensors. 3D operations must also be differentiable so gradients can propagate backward through the system from model output back to the input data. It is especially challenging given that many traditional operators in the computer graphics field, such as rendering, involve steps that block gradients.' Ravi, Gkioxari and Johnson, 'Introducing PyTorch3D'.

81 There are some GANs that operate in 3D, such as 3D-GAN: http://3dgan.csail.mit.edu/.

82 Mike Haley, 'Autodesk, Humans + AO = Future of Designing and Making', *Deep Learning*, Montreal, 7 May 2018, https://www.youtube.com/watch?v=NSJwq9CVolk.

83 Haley, 'Autodesk, Humans + AO'.

84 Kaveh Hassani and Mike Haley, 'Multi-Task Feature Learning on Point Clouds', https://arxiv.org/pdf/1910.08207.pdf.

85 The neural mesh 3D renderer, they note, has the following advantages: 'It is a differentiable rendering/rasterizer algorithm that can be used as an input layer with CNNs and other forms of 2D neural networks. This framework effectively yields a mapping function (the fusion of the differentiable renderer and neural networks) between the 3D polygon mesh and 2D image representation of objects. The Neural 3D Mesh Renderer network is differentiable so the gradients of an image can be taken with respect to the vertices and surfaces of the input mesh. Thus, the same principles/formulations guiding . . . 2D dreaming and 2D style transfer techniques can be used to perform image editing on the surfaces of 3D objects.' Matias del Campo, Sandra Manninger, Alexa Carlson, Marianna Sanche and Leetee Jane Wang, 'Machine Hallucinations: An Examination of Architecture in a Postdigital Design Ecology', International Association for Shell and Spatial Structures, 2019.

86 Stanislas Chaillou, 'The Advent of Architectural AI', *Towards Data Science*, 17 September 2019, https://towardsdatascience.com/the-advent-of-architectural-ai-706046960140.

87 This is not dissimilar to how Gehry Technologies customised Catia – a software developed initially in-house by aircraft manufacturer Dassault Systems to produce its Mirage fighter jet – to produce Digital Project, a computer aided design (CAD) and building informational modelling (BIM) application to be used by architects.

88 One way to resolve this issue, however, is to transform the image from a raster image to a vector format.

89 The term 'style' is highly controversial in architectural circles. Few architects think that they design in a particular style, just as few people think that they speak with an accent. This is because the way we design or speak constitutes our background horizon of consciousness, and we are therefore unaware of it. However, there is a worrying tendency on the part of architectural historians, to read even digital design in terms of style. This can be traced back to publications such as *The Digital Turn*, a collection of essays edited by Mario Carpo, where Carpo interprets the digital as a 'style' based on curvilinear forms, growing out of the work of Greg Lynn and Bernard Cache. Mario Carpo, *The Digital Turn in Architecture 1992–2012*, London: Wiley, 2013. As we know, however, the digital has a far longer and richer history than this, and is not associated with any particular style. Although the digital offers certain affordances, it has no agency. For the theory of affordances, see James Gibson, *The Ecological Approach to Visual Perception*, Hove: Psychology Press, 1979.

3 John Fuegi and Jo Francis, 'Lovelace & Babbage and the creation of the 1843 "notes"', *Annals of the History of Computing* 25, no. 4 (October–December 2003): 16–26.

4 Alan Turing, 'On Computable Numbers, with an Application to the Entscheidungsproblem', *Proceedings of the London Mathematical Society* s2–42, no. 1 (1937): 230–65, doi:10.1112/plms/s2-42.1.230; s2–43, no. 1 (1938): 544–6, doi:10.1112/plms/s2-43.6.544.

5 Andrew Hodges, *Alan Turing: The Enigma*, New York: Princeton University Press, 2012.

6 This scene is played out in the movie *The Imitation Game*. Morten Tyldum (director), *The Imitation Game*, film, 2014.

7 Dermot Turing, *Alan Turing: The Life of a Genius*, Norwich: Pitkin, 2017.

8 Liat Clark and Ian Steadman, 'Remembering Alan Turing: From Codebreaking to AI, Turing made the world we live in today', *Wired*, 7 June 2017, https://www.wired.co.uk/article/turing-contributions.

9 Jack Copeland, *Turing: Pioneer of the Information Age*, Oxford: Oxford University Press, 2012, p. 196.

10 Copeland, *Turing*, p. 198.

11 Technically the race was the Amateur Athletics Association (AAA) championships, but this was effectively the English Championships. It should be noted that Turing's time was only ten minutes slower than the winning time for the men's marathon at the 1948 Olympic Games in London. Turing had intended to run in the British Olympic Trials, but developed a hip injury. Copeland, *Turing*, p. 136; Pat Butcher, 'Record Breaker', *Runner's World*, September 1999, pp. 56–7.

12 Turing, 'Computing Machinery and Intelligence'.

13 'The Turing Test, 1950', *The Alan Turing Internet Scrapbook*, https://www.turing.org.uk/scrapbook/test.html.

14 If Turing remained largely unknown until his exploits were finally revealed, there are many other individuals – especially the female assistants on the projects in which Turing was involved – who remain almost completely unknown even to this day. Kate Lewis, 'Bletchley Park: No Longer the World's Best Kept Secret', *BBC News*, 18 June 2014. See also Sadie Plant, *Zeros and Ones: Digital Women and the New Technoculture*, London: Fourth Estate, 1998.

15 Tyldum, *The Imitation Game*.

16 This was a quote by Turing in *The Times* newspaper in 1949. He was referring to an early computer called the 'mechanical mind' rather than to AI as such. Dermot Turing, *Prof: Alan Turing Decoded*,

Norwich: Pitkin, 2015, https://quoteinvestigator.com/2019/10/12/
ai-shadow.

17 Benjamin Bratton, 'Outing AI: Beyond the Turing Test', *New York
Times*, 23 February 2015.

18 Estimates as to the number of lives that Turing managed to save
through his invention vary widely. Colin Drury estimates that he
saved two million lives. Colin Drury, 'Alan Turing, the father of
modern computing, credited with saving millions of lives',
Independent, 15 July 2019, https://www.independent.co.uk/news/
uk/home-news/alan-turing-50-note-computers-maths-enigma-
codebreaker-ai-test-a9005266.html. But Jack Copeland argues
that the figure might have been as high as 21 million. Jack
Copeland, 'Alan Turing: the codebreaker who saved "millions of
lives"', *BBC News*, 19 June 2012, https://www.bbc.com/news/
technology-18419691.

19 Steve Tribe, *Doctor Who: A Brief History of Time Lords*, New York:
Harper Design, 2017.

20 This, however, is extremely unlikely. The first episode of Dr Who
was broadcast in 1963, at which point Turing's wartime exploits
were still classified as state secrets. However, the linear perception
of time does not necessarily apply to a Time Lord such as Dr Who.

21 Warren McCulloch and Walter Pitts, 'A Logical Calculus of The Ideas
Immanent in Nervous Activity', *Bulletin of Mathematical Biophysics*
5 (1943): 115–33.

22 Babbage, Lovelace, Turing, Ashby, Russell and Sherrington were all
from the United Kingdom, which played a major role in the early
development of computation.

23 Boden, *AI*, p. 10.

24 One of the central figures in the field of cybernetics was Gordon
Pask, who taught at the Architectural Association for several years.
For his essay on cybernetics and architecture, see Gordon Pask,
'The Architectural Relevance of Cybernetics', in Achim Menges and
Sean Alquist (eds), *Computational Design Thinking*, London: Wiley,
2011.

25 Boden, *AI*, p. 17.

26 James Moor, 'The Dartmouth College Artificial Intelligence
Conference: The Next Fifty Years', *AI Magazine* 27, no. 4, (2006):
87–9.

27 J. McCarthy, M. Minsky, N. Rochester and C. E. Shannon, 'A
Proposal for the Dartmouth Summer Research Project on Artificial
Intelligence', August 1955, http://raysolomonoff.com/dartmouth/
boxa/dart564prop.pdf

28 N. J. Nielson, *John McCarthy: A Biographical Memoir*, Washington, DC: National Academy of Sciences, 2012.

29 Marvin Minsky, *Computation: Finite and Infinite Machines*, Englewood Cliffs, NJ: Prentice-Hall, 1967, p. 2.

30 Daniel Crevier, *AI: The Tumultuous Search for Artificial Intelligence*, New York: Basic Books, 1993, p. 203.

31 Russell and Norvig, *Artificial Intelligence*, p. 21.

32 Professor Sir James Lighthill, 'Artificial Intelligence: A General Survey', in *Artificial Intelligence: a paper symposium*, n.p.p.: Science Research Council, 1973.

33 Marvin Minsky and Seymour Papert, *Perceptrons: An Introduction to Computational Geometry*, Cambridge, MA: MIT Press, 1969; Crevier, *AI*, pp. 102–5.

34 Etham Alpaydin defines the perceptron as follows: 'A perceptron is a type of a neural network organized in layers where each layer receives connections from units in the previous layer and feeds its output to units in the layer that follows.' Ethem Alpaydin, *Machine Learning*, Cambridge, MA: MIT Press, 2016, p. 179.

35 Frank Rosenblatt, *Principles of Neurodynamics*, Washington, DC: Spartan Books, 1962.

36 Boden, *AI*, p. 94. For further reading, see Mikel Olazaran, 'A Sociological Study of the Official History of the Perceptrons Controversy', *Social Studies of Science* 26, no. 3 (1996): 611–59. See also Crevier, *AI*, pp. 102–5.

37 Russell in Ford, *Architects of Intelligence*, p. 83.

38 LISP machines were general purpose computers running on LISP software. LISP is an anchronym for Locator/Identifier Separation Protocol. See H. P. Newquist, *The Brain Makers*, Indianapolis: Sams Publishing, 1994.

39 Ray Kurzweil, *The Singularity is Near*, New York: Viking, 2005, p. 264.

40 Kurzweil, *The Singularity is Near*, p. 263.

41 'The History of Chess AI', *Medium*, 28 February 2019, https://becominghuman.ai/the-history-of-chess-ai-f8b0dcb4d6d4.

42 Feng-Hsiung Hsu, *Behind Deep Blue: Building the Computer that Defeated the World Chess Champion*, Princeton, NJ: Princeton University Press, 2002.

43 Peter H. Diamandis, 'Ray Kurzweil's Mind-Boggling Predictions for the Next 25 Years', *Medium*, 22 August 2018, https://medium.com/@singularity_41680/ray-kurzweils-mind-boggling-predictions-for-the-next-25-years-ce3c9163588b.

44 One of the key computational minds behind the project, Taiwanese-American computer scientist Feng-hsiung Hsu, had named one of his earlier computer chess-playing systems 'Deep Thought'. Presumably this was inspired by Deep Thought, the mega-computer that appears in the book, novel and film *The Hitchhiker's Guide to the Galaxy*. Deep Thought had been programmed to answer 'The Ultimate Question to Life, the Universe and Everything'. After 7.5 million years, Deep Thought comes up with the answer '42'. The final name, Deep Blue, was also informed by IBM's nickname, 'Big Blue'. Hsu, *Behind Deep Blue*.

45 Walsh, *Machines that Think*, p. 118.

46 Michelle McPhee, K. C. Baker and Cory Siemaszko, 'Deep Blue, IBM's supercomputer, defeats chess champion Garry Kasparov in 1997', *New York Daily News*, 10 May 2015, https://www.nydailynews.com/news/world/kasparov-deep-blues-losingchess-champ-rooke-article-1.762264.

47 Albert Silver, 'Deep Blue's Cheating Move, *Chess News*, 19 February 2015, https://en.chessbase.com/post/deep-blue-s-cheating-move. This is not surprising, perhaps, given the history of fake chess-playing automata, such as the Mechanical Turk, which was in fact controlled by an dwarf operative, hidden in a cabinet underneath the chess board. Simon Schaffer, 'Enlightened Automata', in William Clark et al. (eds), *The Sciences in Enlightened Europe*, Chicgao and London: University of Chicago Press, 1999, pp. 126–65.

48 Gary Kasparov, 'The Day that I Sensed a New Kind of Intelligence,' *Time* 13, 25 March 1996.

49 Gary Kasparov, *Deep Thinking*, Boston: PublicAffairs, 2017.

50 Gary Kasparov in Elena Holodny, 'One of the greatest chess players of all time, Garry Kasparov, talks about artificial intelligence and the interplay between machine learning and humans', *Business Insider*, 24 May 2017, https://www.businessinsider.com/garry-kasparov-interview-2017-5.

51 Russell in Ford, *Architects of Intelligence*, p. 44.

52 David Ferrucci, Eric Brown, Jennifer Chu-Carroll, James Fan, David Gondek, Aditya A. Kalyanpur, Adam Lally, J. William Murdock, Eric Nyberg, John Prager, Nico Schlaefer and Chris Welty, 'Building Watson: An Overview of the DeepQA Project', *AI Magazine* (Fall, 2010), http://www.aaai.org/Magazine/Watson/watson.php.

53 Mike Hale, 'Actors and their. Hal? Hal!', *New York Times*, 8 February 2011. The challenge was reportedly floated at a dinner between IBM executives, when they noticed that the occupants of an entire restaurant had shifted to be in front of television screens so that they could watch the latest episode of *Jeopardy!*, a television quiz show that had captivated the popular imagination. Stephen Baker, *Final Jeopardy: Man vs Machine and the Quest to Know Everything*, New York: Houghton Mifflin Harcourt, 2011, pp. 6–8.

54 Nonetheless, Watson was able to draw upon a host of sources, including encyclopedias, dictionaries and literary works, although it did not access the internet.

55 An adapted version of IBM's existing question answering system – although good for its time – proved singularly inadequate for Jeopardy! quiz questions. In an early test, for example, the system could only answer 62% of the questions, and only 13% of these answers were correct. Sean Gerrish, *How Smart Machines Think*, Cambridge, MA: MIT Press, 2018, p. 177.

56 Despite its name, DeepQA has nothing to do with deep learning. Gerrish, *How Smart Machines Think*, p. 178.

57 'Watson Crowned Jeopardy King', *BBC News*, 17 Feb 2011, https://www.bbc.com/news/technology-12491688; John Markoff, 'Computer Wins on Jeopardy? Trivial, Its' Not', *New York Times*, 16 February 2011, https://www.nytimes.com/2011/02/17/science/17jeopardy-watson.html.

58 Ken Jennings, 'My Puny Human Brain', *Slate Magazine*, 16 February 2011, https://slate.com/culture/2011/02/watson-jeopardy-computer-ken-jennings-describes-what-it-s-like-to-play-against-a-machine.html.

59 Markoff, 'Computer Wins on Jeopardy?'.

60 Christopher Moyer, 'How Google's AlphaGo Beat a Go World Champion', *Atlantic*, 18 March 2016, https://www.theatlantic.com/technology/archive/2016/03/the-invisible-opponent/475611/.

61 David Silver et al., 'Mastering the game of Go with deep neural networks and tree search', *Nature* 529, 28 January 2016, pp. 484–9.

62 Demis Hassabis, as quoted in Sam Byford, 'DeepMind founder Demis Hassabis on how AI will shape the future', *The Verge*, 10 March 2016.

63 Russell in Ford, *Architects of Intelligence*, 2018, p. 43.

64 Cade Metz, 'The Sadness and Beauty of Watching Google's AI Play Go', *Wired*, 11 March 2011.

65 Christopher Moyer, 'How Google's AlphaGo Beat a Go World Champion', *Atlantic*, 18 March 2016, https://www.theatlantic.com/technology/archive/2016/03/the-invisible-opponent/475611/.

66 Metz, 'The Sadness and Beauty'.

67 Greg Kohs (director), *AlphaGo*, 2017, https://www.alphagomovie.com/.

68 Moyer, 'How Google's AlphaGo Beat a Go World Champion'.

69 Demis Hassabis and Fan Hui, 'AlphaGo: Moving Beyond the Rules', in Woods, Livingston and Uchida, *AI: More Than Human*, p. 89.

70 Hassabis and Hui, 'AlphaGo', p. 84.

71 Kohs, *AlphaGo*.

72 The question is also thrown into relief, as we shall see, by architectural designs generated by AI that expose the limitations of those designed by humans. See p. 122.

73 The AlphaGo project actually consisted of a series of variations of the same programme, starting with the initial AlphaGo version used in a match against European Go champion Fan Hui, in October 2015, then improved to AlphaGo Lee for a match against Sedol in March 2016.

74 Demis Hassabis and David Silver, 'AlphaGo Zero: Learning from Scratch', 18 October 2017, https://deepmind.com/blog/article/alphago-zero-starting-scratch.

75 Merritt Kennedy, 'Computer Learns to Play Go at Superhuman Levels "Without Human Knowledge"', *The Two Way*, 18 October 2017, https://www.npr.org/sections/thetwo-way/2017/10/18/558519095/computer-learns-to-play-go-at-superhuman-levels-without-human-knowledge.

76 David Silver et al., 'Mastering Chess and Shogi by Self-Play with a General Reinforcement Learning Algorithm', 5 December 2017, https://arxiv.org/abs/1712.01815.

77 The AlphaStar Team, 'AlphaStar: Grandmaster level in StarCraft II using multi-agent reinforcement learning', *DeepMind Blog*, 30 October 2019, https://deepmind.com/blog/article/AlphaStar-Grandmaster-level-in-StarCraft-II-using-multi-agent-reinforcement-learning.

78 'Go master Lee says he quits unable to win over AI Go players', Yonhap News Agency, 27 November 2017, https://en.yna.co.kr/view/AEN20191127004800315.

79 Kohs, *AlphaGo*.

80 Kai-Fu Lee, *AI Superpowers: China, Silicon Valley and the New World Order*, New York: Houghton Mifflin Harcourt, 2018, p. 3.

81 Tom Simonite, 'Tencent Software Beats Go Champ, Showing China's AI Gains', *Wired*, 23 January 2018, https://www.wired.com/story/tencent-software-beats-go-champ-showing-chinas-ai-gains/.

82 As NASA observes, 'In general, Kennedy felt great pressure to have the United States "catch up to and overtake" the Soviet Union in the "space race." Four years after the Sputnik shock of 1957, the cosmonaut Yuri Gagarin had become the first human in space on

April 12, 1961, greatly embarrassing the U.S. While Alan Shepard became the first American in space on May 5, he only flew on a short suborbital flight instead of orbiting the Earth, as Gagarin had done.' As quoted in Neil Leach, 'Terrestrial Feedback', in Neil Leach (ed.), 'Space Architecture: The New Frontier for Design Research, *AD*, Profile No. 232, November/December 2014.

83 Paul Mozur comments, 'The two professors who consulted with the government on A.I. both said that the 2016 defeat of Lee Sedol, a South Korean master of the board game Go, by Google's AlphaGo had a profound impact on politicians in China . . . As a sort of Sputnik moment for China, the professors said, the event paved the way for a new flow of funds into the discipline.' Paul Mozur, 'Beijing Wants A.I. to Be Made in China by 2030', *New York Times*, 20 July 2017, https://www.nytimes.com/2017/07/20/business/china-artificial-intelligence.html.

84 Nicholas Thomson and Ian Bremner, 'The AI Cold War That Threatens Us All', *Wired*, 23 October 2018, https://www.wired.com/story/ai-cold-war-china-could-doom-us-all/.

85 Fu-Lee continues: 'When the Soviet Union launched the first human-made satellite into orbit in October 1957, it had an instant and profound effect on the American psyche and government policy. The event sparked widespread US public anxiety about perceived Soviet technological superiority, with Americans following the satellite across the night sky and tuning into Sputnik's radio transmissions. It triggered the formation of the National Aeronautical Space Administration (NASA), fueled major government subsidies for math and science education, and effectively launched the space race. Lee, *AI Superpowers*.

86 Carissa Schoenick, 'China May Overtake US in AI Research', *Medium*, 13 March 2019, https://medium.com/ai2-blog/china-to-overtake-us-in-ai-research-8b6b1fe30595.

87 Lee, *AI Superpowers*, p. 227.

88 Lee, *AI Superpowers*, p. 4.

89 Mark Zastrow, 'South Korea trumpets $860-million AI fund after AlphaGo "shock"', *Nature*, 18 March 2016, https://www.nature.com/news/south-korea-trumpets-860-million-ai-fund-after-alphago-shock-1.19595.

90 Metz, 'The Sadness and Beauty'.

91 Demis Hassabis and Fan Hui, 'Exploring the Mysteries of Go with AlphaGo and top Chinese Go Players', *DeepMind Blog Research*, 10 April 2017, https://deepmind.com/blog/article/exploring-mysteries-alphago.

92 Chris Weller, 'Meet the first-ever robot citizen – a humanoid robot named Sophia that once said that it would 'destroy humans', *Business Insider*, 27 October 2017, https://www.businessinsider.com/meet-the-first-robot-citizen-sophia-animatronic-humanoid-2017-10?r=UK.

93 'UNDP in Asia and the Pacific Appoints World's First Non-Human Innovation Champion', *UNDP Asia and the Pacific*, 22 November 2017.

94 Lana Sinapayen, 'Sophia the Robot, More Marketing Machine than AI Marvel', *Skynet Today*, 20 November 2018. https://www.skynettoday.com/briefs/sophia.

95 In the past there have been examples of people masquerading as an automaton, as in the case of the Mechanical Turk, an 'automaton' that was actually operated by a chess-playing dwarf hidden underneath. Tom Standage, *The Turk: The Life and Times of the Famous Eighteenth-Century Chess-Playing Machine*, New York: Walker, 2002.

96 Zoom conversation, 6 May 2020.

97 This was revealed to me by David Mallard, CEO of AI SpaceFactory, at a conference in Shanghai in September 2019, https://www.aispacefactory.com/.

98 This is a reference to the famous expression, 'Beware the Ides of March!', from the play by Shakespeare, *Julius Caesar*, Act 1, Scene 2 (1599), http://www.online-literature.com/shakespeare/julius_caesar/3/.

Chapter 3

1 Ada Lovelace, Notes (on the Analytical Engine), 1843.

2 Lovelace, Notes.

3 Teri Perl, '*The Ladies Diary* or *Woman's Almanac*, 1704–1841', *Historica Mathematica* 6 (1979): 36–53.

4 For further discussion on this, see Marcus du Sautoy, *The Creativity Code: Art and Innovation in the Age of AI*, Cambridge, MA: Harvard University Press, 2019.

5 This, of course, is an open question. We have no answer to it as yet. And much depends on whether 'thinking' involves consciousness. If it does, then machines cannot literally think, at least until we reach AGI. Turing, 'Computing Machinery and Intelligence'.

6 Turing adds an interesting qualification, surmising that human beings might not be able to fully appreciate these sonnets: 'Though the comparison is perhaps a little bit unfair, because a sonnet written by a machine will be better appreciated by another machine.' Dermot Turing, *Prof.*

7 Turing, 'Computing Machinery and Intelligence'.

8 Turing, 'Computing Machinery and Intelligence'. The unpredictability of computers is potentially the biggest danger in using machine learning algorithms. As Memo Akten observes, 'This is precisely where potentially the biggest dangers of using machine learning algorithms lie. Especially with regards to *algorithmic decision making in critical situations*, and partly why we're having the problems we have today – because we're unable to predict how the trained algorithms might behave, and we can't hold them accountable. But simultaneously, this is also the biggest advantage of machine learning systems. This is how machines can potentially help propel us to new places, to make us *see things that we otherwise wouldn't be able to see.*' Memo Akten, 'Retune 2016, Part 2: Algorithmic Decision Making, Machine Bias, Creativity and Diversity', *Medium*, 14 October 2016, https://medium.com/@memoakten/retune-2016-part-2-algorithmic-decision-making-machine-bias-creativity-and-diversity-3c7cca21ba37.

9 Richard Susskind and Daniel Susskind, *The Future of the Professions: How Technology will Transform the Work of Human Experts*, Oxford: Oxford University Press, 2015, p. xi.

10 Mitchell, *Artificial Intelligence*, p. 272.

11 The question of consciousness in relation to extended intelligence is addressed further in the next chapter.

12 At the time of writing, when asked the question, 'Alexa, would you say that you are creative?' Alexa replies, 'Sorry. I'm not sure.'

13 Blaise Agüera y Arcas, 'What is AMI?', *Medium*, 23 February 2016, https://medium.com/artists-and-machine-intelligence/what-is-ami-96cd9ff49dde.

14 For an overview of artists using AI, see https://aiartists.org/.

15 Alex Rayner, 'Can Google's Deep Dream become an art machine?', *Guardian*, 28 March 2016, https://www.theguardian.com/artanddesign/2016/mar/28/google-deep-dream-art.

16 Joanna Zylinska, *AI Art: Machine Visions and Warped Dreams*, London: Open Humanities Press, 2020, p. 50.

17 Is artificial intelligence set to become art's next medium? https://www.christies.com/features/A-collaboration-between-two-artists-one-human-one-a-machine-9332-1.aspx.

18 James Vincent, 'How Three French Students used Borrowed Code to Put the First AI Portrait in Christie's, *The Verge*, 23 October 2018, https://www.theverge.com/2018/10/23/18013190/ai-art-portrait-auction-christies-belamy-obvious-robbie-barrat-gans.

19 It could also be argued, however, that AI could fail the Turing Test if it shows itself to be too knowledgeable and display a level of knowledge beyond what might be expected of a human being. Hussan Hamden, 'Both Turing Test and GAN Attempt to Fool a Judge', 1 November 2019, *Medium*, https://medium.com/@hamdan.hussam/both-turing-test-and-gan-attempt-to-fool-a-judge-7391665ffca2.

20 https://lumenprize.com/artwork/the-butchers-son/.

21 Martin Dean, 'Artist Mario Klingemann on Artificial Intelligence, Technology and our Future' (interview with Mario Klingemann), Sotheby's, 25 February 2019, https://www.sothebys.com/en/articles/artist-mario-klingemann-on-artificial-intelligence-art-tech-and-our-future.

22 'Art and Artificial Intelligence Laboratory at Rutgers: Advancing AI Technology in the Digital Humanities', https://sites.google.com/site/digihumanlab/home.

23 Ian Bogost, 'The AI-Art Gold Rush is Here', *Atlantic*, 6 March 2019.

24 Taesung Park, Ming-Yu Liu, Ting-Chun Wang and Jun-Yan Zhu. 'Semantic Image Synthesis with Spatially-Adaptive Normalization', *CVPR*, 2019, https://arxiv.org/pdf/1903.07291.pdf.

25 'GauGAN Wins Major Awards at SIGGRAPH 2019's Real Time Live Competition', Nvidiia Developer News Center, 30 July 2019, https://news.developer.nvidia.com/gaugan-wins-major-awards-at-siggraph-2019s-real-time-live-competition/.

26 'GauGAN Wins Major Awards'.

27 The parallel here is with the simple mobile phone. Intended initially for wealthy businessmen, the mobile phone became a viable product from a marketing perspective once those businessmen started giving phones to other family members so that they could call them and have them pick them up in the evening.

28 https://medium.com/artists-and-machine-intelligence/what-is-ami-ccd936394a83.

29 Walter Benjamin, *The Work of Art in the Age of Mechanical Reproduction*, Scottsdale, AZ: Prism Key Press, 2010.

30 This had ramifications in the recent intriguing case involving monkeys and David Slater, a wildlife photographer. Slater gave his

2   *Blade Runner* was set on 19–21 November 2019, as we find out in
the sequel, *Blade Runner 2049*.

3   The dream of the unicorn, and the origami figures of unicorns made
by Gaff, a police officer with the LAPD in *Blade Runner*, have been
cited as reasons why Deckard himself might be a replicant, a
possibility left dangling as a fascinating idea in *Blade Runner*, and
confirmed as being correct in *Blade Runner 2049*. Murray Chapman,
'What is the significance of the unicorn?', *Blade Runner Insights*,
1998, https://br-insight.com/library/significance-of-the-unicorn/.

4   Makoto Sei Watanabe, 'AI Tect: Can AI Make Designs?', in Neil
Leach and Philip Yuan (eds), *Computational Design*, Shanghai:
Tongji University Press, 2017, pp. 68–75. Tracking the development
of AI within the domain of architecture is far from easy. Many
AI researchers post their research on online platforms, such as
Medium. But there is no single site dedicated to research on AI
and architecture. Nor indeed is there any research journal as yet
dedicated to AI and architecture. As such, any overview of
developments in this field risks overlooking some of the key
players, especially when they are publishing their work in
languages other than English.

5   Watanabe, 'AI Tect: Can AI Make Designs?'.

6   www.thispersondoesnotexist.com. The principle lay behind the
architectural website, *This building does not exist* (www.
thisbuildingdoesnotexist.com) which is no longer operative.

7   Kostas Terzidis, *Algorithmic Architecture*, London: Routledge, 2006,
p. 11; Kostas Terzidis, *Permutation Design*, London: Routledge, 2014,
p. 85. This also begins to suggest that certain more conservative
approaches to creativity, such as that of Martin Heidegger, need to
be reconsidered. For example, Heidegger's notion that the work
of art is linked to the Greek term '*aletheia*', which means 'not
forgetting'. In other words, in producing the work of art the 'artist'
merely uncovers – or 'remembers' – an already existing 'truth'. On
this, see Leach, *Rethinking Architecture*, pp. 98–9.

8   Refik Anadol, 'Art in the Age of Machine Intelligence', TED Talk, July
2020, https://www.ted.com/talks/refik_anadol_art_in_the_age_of_
machine_intelligence/transcript?language=en.

9   Refik Anadol, 'DigitialFUTURES: AI and Neuroscience', 6 July 2020,
https://www.youtube.com/watch?v=L1H7eL8pk5k&list=PLtuu5idZ5
7EUn4j0H3a95ksa6PzJYq11x&index=10.

10   This comment was originally made by Koolhaas as a first-year
student at the AA in an essay for Elia Zengelis. Rem Koolhaas,
Stefano Boeri, Sanford Kwinter, Nadia Tazi and Hans Ulrich Obrist,
Mutations, Barcelona: Actar, 2000.

11 Koolhaas et al., *Mutations*.

12 Yonca Keremoglu, 'A Data Universe Made of Memories, AI and Architecture', interview with Refik Anadol, *Digicult*, undated, http:// digicult.it/articles/a-data-universe-made-of-memories-ai-and-architecture-interview-with-refik-anadol/.

13 Anadol, 'DigitialFUTURES'.

14 Anadol, 'Art in the Age of Machine Intelligence'.

15 Google Arts and Culture, 2018, 'WDCH Dreams', https:// artsandculture.google.com/exhibit/wdch-dreams-laphil/ yQIyh25RSGAtLg?hl=en.

16 Anadol, 'Art in the Age of Machine Intelligence'.

17 Understood in human terms, then, 'memory', 'dream' and 'consciousness' have to be presented here in inverted commas. AI does not literally possess the kinds of memories, dreams or consciousness that human beings possess. Anil Seth, however, notes that the precise meaning depends on its context. When we use the term 'memory' as in computer memory or memory mattress, do we need to put it in inverted commas? Anil Seth, 'DigitialFUTURES: AI and Neuroscience', 6 July 2020, https://www. youtube.com/watch?v=L1H7eL8pk5k&list=PLtuu5idZ57EUn4j0H3a 95ksa6PzJYq11x&index=10.

18 The theme of memory builds upon the earlier project by Anadol, *Melting Memories*, http://refikanadol.com/works/melting-memories/.

19 As Anadol notes, 'We take every folder, every image, every sound recording in the archive, one by one, and let the archive load itself into a RAM or buffer so the building goes through its nostalgic folders, finds the first music directors, finds the first iconic moments in time, and the building plots them for us.' Kyle Huewe, 'Refik Anadol: "WDCH Dreams"', *Flaunt*, 20 November 2018, www. flaunt.com/content/refik-anadol.

20 'The second part,' notes Anadol, 'is completely organic. The building starts to look at its own entire history. Suddenly, we see a bunch of Big Bang moments. Data universes appear in front of us, as emotional as possible.' Huewe, 'Refik Anadol'.

21 Huewe, 'Refik Anadol'.

22 This was not Anadol's first project connected with the WCDH. His *Visions of America* (2014) was an interactive installation projected on to the interior of the concert hall, http://refikanadol.com/works/ visions-of-america-ameriques/.

23 Anadol, 'DigitialFUTURES'.

24 Anadol, 'DigitialFUTURES'.

25 'When I think of it, *Infinity Room* stems from a childish memory. As a child, I used to dream about transforming places a lot. Though I used to play with Army Men and toy cars as an alternative, I did weird things with the spatial elements of the house such as creating a place in the attic of our house or re-designing the window of the room. In fact, my mom had considered taking me to the psychologist as my interests differed from conventional methods of a play. I always dreamed about changing and transforming spaces, and *Infinity Room* was actually the output of those dreams.' Susan Fourtané, 'Refik Anadol: The Leonardo da Vinci of the 21st Century', *Interesting Engineering*, 23 June 2019, https://interestingengineering.com/refik-anadol-the-leonardo-da-vinci-of-the-21st-century.

26 https://refikanadol.com/works/wind-of-boston-data-paintings/; https://refikanadol.com/works/bosphorus/.

27 https://www.artechouse.com/nyc.

28 On occasions, however, Anadol himself did intervene in order to heighten the effect: 'Basically, as an artist I took my brush, and stuck it into the machine's mind and paint architecture with the machine's consciousness.' See Bruce Sterling, 'Refik Anadol at Artechouse in New York City', *Wired*, 30 October 2019.

29 The image was generated as part of a series of investigations into StyleGANs focused initially on the various stylistic eras, e.g. Gothic, Renaissance, Modernism, Deconstructivism, and then on the works of particular architects, such as Gehry and Partners, ZHA, Toyo Ito and Tadao Ando.

30 However, we should be conscious of the risk of anthropomorphising computer operations by using human-centric language to describe their operations.

31 Indeed, according to neuroscientist, Anil Seth, our whole notion of colour is itself a construct, generated by the brain: 'DigitalFUTURES'.

32 Seth, 'A predictive processing theory of sensorimotor contingencies', 97–118; Clark, *Surfing Uncertainty*.

33 Seth, 'A predictive processing theory of sensorimotor contingencies', 97–118 . This is not dissimilar to the 'double moment of vision' that Christian Metz describes (Christian Metz, *Psychoanalysis and the Cinema*, London: Macmillan, 1992, p. 51): 'As one casts one's eye (in a projective fashion), one receives and absorbs (in an introjective fashion) what has been "illuminated", as it were.' Consciousness therefore serves, in Metz's terminology, as a "recording surface". Leach, *Camouflage*, pp. 140–1.

34 Seth and his team have explored how altered states of consciousness help us to understand underlying conscious perception: Keisuke Suzuki, Warrick Roseboom, David J. Schwartzman and Anil K. Seth, 'A Deep-Dream Virtual Reality Platform for Studying Altered Perceptual Phenomenology', *Scientific Reports* 7, no. 15982 (2017), DOI:10.1038/s41598-017-16316-2.

35 Rick Grush has previously used the notion of 'controlled hallucination'. Grush acknowledges, however, that the expression had been coined originally by Ramesh Jain in a talk at UCSD. Rick Grush, 'The Emulation Theory of Representation: Motor Control, Imagery, and Perception', *Behavioral and Brain Sciences* 27 (2004): 377–442 (p. 393).

36 Anil Seth, 'Your Brain Hallucinates Your Conscious Reality', TED Talk, April 2017, https://www.ted.com/talks/anil_seth_your_brain_hallucinates_your_conscious_reality?language=en.

37 Memo Akten, 'Learning to See: Gloomy Sunday', 2017, Memo.tv. http://www.memo.tv/portfolio/gloomy-sunday/.

38 Akten, 'Learning to See: Gloomy Sunday'.

39 *Jouissance* is the bittersweet moment that flares up in aesthetic contemplation. See Leach, *Camouflage*, p. 232. See also Dylan Evans, *An Introductory Dictionary of Lacanian Psychoanalysis*, London: Routledge, 1996, p. 92.

40 'This is precisely what Lacan has in mind when he says that fantasy is the ultimate support of reality: "reality" stabilizes itself when some fantasy-frame of a "symbolic bliss" forecloses the view into the abyss of the Real.' Slavoj Zizek, 'From Virtual Reality to the Virtualisation of Reality', in Leach, *Designing for a Digital World*, p. 122.

41 This is somewhat different to the interpretation of Seth, who argues that 'reality' is a form of consensus as to what we see, when we agree about our controlled hallucinations. Seth, 'Your Brain Hallucinates Your Conscious Reality'.

42 Zizek, 'From Virtual Reality to the Virtualisation of Reality', p. 122.

43 Zizek, 'From Virtual Reality to the Virtualisation of Reality', p. 123.

44 Nic Bostrom, 'Are You Living in a Computer Simulation?', *Philosophical Quarterly* 53, no. 211 (2003): 243–55.

45 Zizek, 'From Virtual Reality to the Virtualisation of Reality', p. 125.

46 https://www.youtube.com/watch?v=WCsjbPc9624&feature=youtu.be.

47 This experiment could be compared, perhaps, to the artistic strategy of making some random mark – a splash of paint or pencil lines – in order to start generating an artwork. In his text, *Francis Bacon: The*

diminish certain features that the network sees or that the network outputs. This is not to say that we don't build different datasets. For all the buildings that we render, we also create clean 3D models that are organized with one unifying strategy.' WhatsApp conversation.

26 Thom Mayne, interview in Chandler Ahrens and Aaron Sprecher (eds), *Instabilities and Potentialities: Notes on the Nature of Knowledge in Digital Architecture*, New York: Routledge, 2019, p. 115.

27 Mayne, interview in Ahrens and Sprecher, *Instabilities and Potentialities*, p. 117.

28 Mayne, interview in Ahrens and Sprecher, *Instabilities and Potentialities*, p. 117.

29 Mayne, interview in Ahrens and Sprecher, *Instabilities and Potentialities*, p. 117.

30 Interview with Thom Mayne, Morphosis office, 27 February 2020.

31 Interview with Mayne, Morphosis office.

32 Interview with Mayne, Morphosis office.

33 Grasshopper here could be understood as a simple form of AI, just as AI for some people could simply be understood as software.

34 Neuroscientist Antonio Damasio describes intuition as 'the mysterious mechanism by which we arrive at a solution of a problem without reasoning toward it'. Antonio Damasio, *Descartes' Error: Emotion, Reason, and the Human Brain*, New York: Putnam, 1994, p. 188.

35 Watanabe, 'AI Tect: Can AI Make Designs?', p. 68.

36 Watanabe: 'If these processes can be written as algorithms, they can be translated into computer programs. And if programs can be written, they can be used to generate architecture. Therefore, the core of this method is the externalization of algorithms.' This is what leads Watanabe to explore the notion of what he calls the 'AI Tect': 'The word AI Tect encompasses two meanings: Architectural Intelligence and Artificial Intelligence.' Watanabe, 'AI Tect: Can AI Make Designs?', p. 70.

37 Watanabe, 'AI Tect: Can AI Make Designs?', p. 71.

38 Satoru Sugihara, 'Design Outside of the Frame: A Role of Architects in the Era of Artificial Intelligence,' in Chandler Ahrens and Aaron Sprecher (eds), *Instabilities and Potentialities: Notes on the Nature of Knowledge in Digital Architecture*, London: Routledge, 2019, p.178.

39 Patrik Schumacher, 'Comment Intégrez-Vous l'IA dans vos Travaux?', *Ircam*, 21 February 2020, https://www.youtube.com/watch?v=EFNdJLKufAY.

40 Schumacher, 'Comment Intégrez-Vous l'IA dans vos Travaux?'.

41 Schumacher, 'Comment Intégrez-Vous l'IA dans vos Travaux?'.

42 I am grateful to Daniel Bolojan for information on this research.

43 There are, of course, many other techniques for testing the performance of a building that have not been covered here.

44 Helix Re, for example, makes extensive use of 'digital twins' for testing the performance of buildings. Jim Lichtenwalter, 'Fireside Q&A: Jamie Roche, HELIX RE's CEO', *Builtworlds*, 3 May 2019, https://builtworlds.com/news/fireside-qa-jamie-roche-helix-res-ceo/.

45 There are, of course, many other AI techniques to test out designs, a subject for which there is insufficient space to cover here.

46 We should not overlook, however, the challenges of working with AI, and GANs especially. Nor should we overlook the sheer quantity of GPU resources required to work with deep learning.

47 Russell in Ford, *Architects of Intelligence*, p. 43.

48 Russell in Ford, *Architects of Intelligence*, p. 43.

49 'Although the design and fabrication of . . . architectural forms might involve the use of digital tools, in and of themselves the forms are not digital. There is no such thing as a digital material, if by "digital" we understand the opposite of "analogue". By extension, there cannot be any such thing as digital architecture, if by "architecture" we understand material buildings. This is not to say that there cannot be digital designs of buildings, but these designs are in effect immaterial models.' Leach, 'There Is No Such Thing as a Digital Building', p. 141.

50 As I have noted previously, 'Although there is a continually expanding list of digital fabrication technologies, with new technologies being developed all the time, especially in the area of 3D printing, at their core these processes have existed for millennia. After all, what is brick construction other than a form of additive manufacturing? What are carving, chiseling, and sawing other than forms of subtractive manufacturing? And what are processes, such as the stacking of bricks, bending of pipes, or folding of sheets of lead but analog versions of processes now often undertaken using robotic tools? As such, we might recognize that what digital fabrication can do is – in some senses – nothing new.' Neil Leach, 'Introduction', in Philip Yuan, Achim Menges and Neil Leach, *Digital Fabrication*, Shanghai: TongjiUniversity Press, 2017, p. 13.

51 As Neil Gershenfeld astutely observes, 'What has grown forward is a digital revolution in making things. It's cutting, grinding, lasers, plasmas, jets of water, wires, knives, bending pins, weaving, moulding, extruding, fusing and bonding.' N. Gershenfeld, M. Carney, B. Jenett and S. Wilson, 'Macrofabrication with Digital Tools: Robotic Assembly', *AD* 85, no. 5 (2015): 122–7.

52 In fact the primary role that the digital plays is that of 'control' – whether it be the control of a tool path for a Computer Numerically Controlled (CNC) milling machine, or the control of a curve in the design, or the control of the logistics of design and fabrication through BIM and other software.

53 This is the principle that lies behind AI Build, a start-up in London established by Dahgan Cam and Michail Desyllas, two graduates of the AA DRL programme. Cam and Desyllas have been exploring the use of AI to monitor and control additive manufacturing processes. In particular, they are attempting to reimagine the factory of the future by using AI technologies. Guy Brown, '3 Fundamentals of High-Speed, High-Quality 3D Printing', *Medium*, 23 August 2019, https://medium.com/ai-build-techblog/3-fundamentals-of-high-speed-high-quality-3d-printing-1f9b384cfe70.

54 Rodney Brooks quoted in Ford, *Architects of Intelligence*, p. 435.

55 Daniel Terdiman, 'Autodesk's Lego Model-Building Robot is the Future of Manufacturing', *Fast Company*, 20 July 2018, https://www.fastcompany.com/90204615/autodesks-lego-model-building-robot-is-the-future-of-manufacturing.

Chapter 6

1 Mike Haley, 'The Future of Design Powered by AI', *Autodesk University*, 2019, https://www.autodesk.com/autodesk-university/content/future-design-powered-ai-mike-haley-2019.

2 Elsewhere Haley describes research being undertaken at Autodesk that amounts to a form of 'predictive design', not so dissimilar to predictive text. Mike Haley, 'The Future of Design Powered by AI', https://www.autodesk.com/autodesk-university/content/future-design-powered-ai-mike-haley-2019.

3 This has now become a new line of research at Autodesk, focused on exploring how previous design experiences can feed into future design experiences, using a 'knowledge graph' that mines every design that a designer has created, so as to make suggestions based on knowledge encoded in previous designs. Mike Haley, 'Humans + AI = The Future of Making', Deep Learning Montréal @ Autodesk, 6 May 2018, https://knowledge.autodesk.com/search-result/caas/video/youtube/watch-v-NSJwq9CVolk.html.

4   Randy Deutsch, *Superusers: Design Technology Specialists and the Future of Practice*, London and New York: Routledge, 2019, p. xix.

5   The same situation obviously applies to writing. To make a text easy to read, considerable effort must be made to ensure that the words flow naturally.

6   Mae Rice, 'The Top 21 AI Real Estate Companies to Know', *Built In*, 29 July 2019, https://builtin.com/artificial-intelligence/ai-real-estate.

7   Håvard Haukeland, 'Spacemaker named among world's 500 most innovative science and deep tech startups!', *Medium*, 4 September 2017, https://blog.spacemaker.ai/spacemaker-named-among-worlds-500-most-innovative-science-and-deep-tech-startups-2016618c2c12.

8   Jonas Blick Bakken, 'Gründerbedriften har snart 100 ansatte – pekes ut som det heteste stedet å jobbe', *Dagens Næringsliv*, 27 April 2019; https://www.dn.no/morgendagens-naringsliv/spacemaker/carl-christensen/havard-haukeland/grunderbedriften-har-snart-100-ansatte-pekes-ut-som-det-heteste-stedet-a-jobbe/2-1-577148?fbclid=IwAR2K5NbDjVYFAO1iEPmUJs_MJ6L5Y1R6TOrwCNe4fTCc1agt6am4d9F9Uuw.

9   *Dagens Næringsliv*, https://www.dn.no/staticprojects/2019/01/grundere/?sector=Fintech#/vinnere/oppstart-b2b.

10 Steve O'Hear, 'Spacemaker, AI software for urban development, is acquired by Aurodesk for $240 milllion', *TechCrunch*, 17 November 2020, https://techcrunch-com.cdn.ampproject.org/c/s/techcrunch.com/2020/11/17/spacemaker-ai-software-for-urban-development-is-acquired-by-autodesk-for-240m/amp/.

11 Steve O'Hear, 'Spacemaker Scores $25 million Series A to Let Property Developers Use AI', *TechCrunch*, 9 June 2019, https://techcrunch.com/2019/06/09/spacemaker/.

12 Bilal Chowdhry, 'Designing Better Cities with Artificial Intelligence', *Designing in the Wild*, Interaction 3–8 February 2019, Seattle, Washington, https://interaction19.ixda.org/program/talk-designing-better-cities-with-artificial-intelligence-bilal-chaudhry/.

13 Zoom conversation, 6 May 2020.

14 Klara Vatn, 'Introducing Explore, a creative toolbox for architects and developers', *Medium*, 4 May 2020, https://blog.spacemaker.ai/introducing-explore-a-creative-toolbox-for-architects-and-developers-4d1a8df1318d.

15 Zoom conversation, 6 May 2020.

16 Vatn, 'Introducing Explore'.

17 Carl Christensen, 'Global PropTech Interview #5 with Carl Christensen, co-founder of Spacemaker AI', 2 December 2019, https://www.youtube.com/watch?v=hvmus_VUtQ8&app=desktop. 'Surrogate models' here should be understood as 'digital twins'.

18 Carl Christensen, 'Global PropTech Interview #5'. Isaac Newton claimed that he had 'seen further' by 'standing on the shoulder of giants', by which he meant that he had benefitted from the consolidated knowledge built up in the past. 'Isaac Newton Letter to Robert Hooke, 1675', https://discover.hsp.org/Record/dc-9792/Description#tabnav. Now with AI on our shoulders, we ourselves can become 'giants', or 'superusers' in Deutsch's terms.

19 Zoom conversation, 6 May 2020.

20 Zoom conversation, 6 May 2020.

21 Zoom conversation, 6 May 2020.

22 Zoom conversation, 6 May 2020.

23 Zoom conversation, 6 May 2020.

24 Zoom conversation, 6 May 2020.

25 Zoom conversation, 6 May 2020.

26 https://www.urbandictionary.com/define.php?term=xkool.

27 Article translated using Google Translate from https://www.gooood.cn/job-xkool.htm.

28 At the time of writing, 100 million RMB is the equivalent of approximately US$14 million. See also, 'AI Architectural Design SaaS Firm Xkool Raises RMB 8-digit Pre-A, Marbridge Daily', 20 June 2018, https://www.marbridgeconsulting.com/marbridgedaily/2018-06-20/article/111781/ai_architectural_design_saas_firm_xkool_raises_rmb_8_digit_pre_a.

29 Wanyu He, 'Urban Experiment: Taking off on the wind of AI', *AD* 90, no. 3 (2020): 99.

30 With the 'design brain' there are in fact three different neural networks used to generate the designs. The first, called 'Babel', consists of a rapid generation neural network based on basic design logic; the second, called 'Parthenon', is a convolutional neural network trained on a dataset of a million examples of advanced architectural designs; and the third, called 'Colosseum', is a GAN trained using the 'Parthenon' neural network. Its role is to generate further options that can be evaluated to produce the preferred result. The 'evaluation brain' balances the output of the 'design brain' using a Monte Carlo Tree Search (MCTS). The MCTS keeps repeating four steps – selection, expansion, simulation and backpropagation – until the nine best solutions are achieved. Xi Peng, Pengkun Liu and Yunfeng Jin, 'The Age of Intelligence: Urban Design Thinking, Method Turning and Exploration', 2020, 10.1007/978-981-13-8153-9_25.

31 As He notes, 'The early intelligent design tools, relying heavily on expert systems for machine learning, were developed to improve the calculating efficiency in pre-planning stages with semi-automation technology, in order to help reduce time and labor cost on massive calculation. Essentially, these tools perform to generate all kinds of design possibilities, with no capability to inform designers with a reference.' Wanyu He, 'From Competition, Coexistence to Win–Win Relationship between Intelligent Design Tools and Human Designers', *Landscape Architecture Frontiers* 7, no. 2 (2019): 76–83.

32 'The emergence of supervised learning algorithm based on statistical learning, feature extraction, and optimization techniques, accompanying . . . a series of unsupervised learning algorithms based on deep learning technology, have further improved the running logic of design tools for exploring an approximate optimal solution.' He, 'From Competition, Coexistence to Win–Win Relationship', 76–83.

33 The Rosetta Stone is a stone slab discovered in 1799 and inscribed with three versions of a decree issued in Egypt in 196 BC. One version was in ancient Egyptian hieroglyphic script, one in ancient Egyptian Demootic script and one in ancient Greek script. By comparing these three scripts, researchers were able to decode ancient Egyptian hieroglyphic script for the first time. Richard Parkinson, Whitfield Diffie, Marie Fischer and R. Simpson, *Cracking Codes: The Rosetta Stone and Decipherment*, Berkeley: University of California Press, 1999.

34 He, 'From Competition, Coexistence to Win–Win Relationship', 76–83.

35 He, 'Urban Experiment', pp. 95–9.

36 Xkool developed a multi-dimensional urban digital platform to analyse a typical urban village in Shenzhen for the 2017 Shenzhen–Hong Kong Bi-City Biennale of Urbanism/Archtecture, which ultimately inspired a proposal to revise the layout of rubbish collection facilities. The platform consisted of a recurrent neural network (RNN) and long short-term memory (LSTM) network regression model. He, 'Urban Experiment', pp. 95–9.

37 This was inspired by the platform 'This Person Does not Exist', which was able to hallucinate extremely convincing faces, with only the occasional telltale blemish, https://thispersondoesnotexist.com/.

38 https://eyesofthecity.net/ai-chitect/.

39 'The platform can generate and recommend plans for users' consideration, which will be used for design development. Compared with research based on the shape grammar of Palladian villas and subsequent parametric design research, this platform, together with similar exercises in the urban/architecture field, focuses on tapping machines' creation potential by teaching machines rules through training data instead of setting the rules manually.' He, 'Urban Experiment', p. 99.

40 Christensen comments, 'Our ambition is to make this the *de facto* platform for planning real estate developments in the Nordics, and in Europe and in the world.' Christensen, 'Global PropTech Interview #5'.

41 Zoom conversation, 6 May 2020.

42 Amy Webb, 'China is Leading in Artificial Intelligence, and American Businesses Should Take Note', *Inc.*, September 2018, https://www.inc.com/magazine/201809/amy-webb/china-artificial-intelligence.html.

43 Neil Leach, 'There is No Such Thing as Digital Design', in David Gerber and Mariana Ibanez (eds), *Paradigms in Computing: Making, Machines, and Models for Design Agency in Architecture*, Los Angeles: eVolo Press, 2014, pp. 148–58.

44 This was the process used in the generation of a structural installation at the Academie van Bouwkunst in Amsterdam in 2002, whereby an array of possible 'solutions' were generated computationally by the eifFORM programme according to a given set of constraints through a proprietary process of stochastic non-monotonic simulated annealing. The final version was selected largely on aesthetic grounds. Kristina Shea, 'Directed Randomness', in Neil Leach, David Turnbull and Chris Williams (eds), *Digital Tectonics*, London: Wiley, 2004.

45 I am reminded here of a review at the AA several years ago. One student presented his project, showing us six different design options. The next student had run the problem through a computer and came up with multiple potential solutions. Although most of them looked remarkably similar, he had at least escaped human biases and been more objective in his approach.

46 Autodesk is also exploring the possibility of using AI to overcome human biases. Haley, 'Humans + AI'.

47 Larry Page, 'The Academy of Achievement Interview', www,achievement.org, 28 October 2000, as quoted in Tom Taulli, *Artificial Intelligence Basics: A Non-Technical Introduction*, New York: Apress, 2019, p.1.

48 Wolfram Alpha gives the answer to this question as '42', based on a reference to the question in Douglas Adams, *The Hitchhiker's Guide to the Galaxy*, New York: Pocket Books, 1979, p. 3.

49 For an example, see the interview with Ada Lovelace generated using aiwriter.app: https://aiwriter.app/sample/43ffa2aeb4253fdadc.

50 At the time of writing, Alexa will take you to the Wikipedia page on 'Construction', if this request is made.

Chapter 7

1 Patrik Schumacher, 'Parametricism: A New Global Style for Architecture and Urban Design', in Neil Leach (ed.), 'Digital Cities', *AD* 79, no. 4 (July–August 2009): 15. The article is reprinted in Leach and Yuan, *Computational Design*. See also Nick Pisca, 'Forget Parametricism', in Leach and Yuan, *Computational Design*.

2 Schumacher, 'Parametricism', p. 16.

3 Schumacher, 'Parametricism', p. 15.

4 Nick Pisca offers a critique of parametricism: '[Digitalism] prides itself on the beauty of the logic of a system over the culturally accepted preconceptions of beauty and form. Logic in the new form. Form follows formula.' Nick Pisca, 'Forget Parametricism', in Leach and Yuan, *Computational Design*, pp. 43–8. See also Neil Leach, 'The Informational City', *Next Generation Building* 2 (2015), TU Delft.

5 Even in the recently constructed city of Ordos, we see little evidence of what Schumacher calls 'parametricism', apart from a museum designed by MAD Architects. Ordos is a city that has struggled to succeed. Peter Day, 'Ordos: The Biggest Ghost Town in China', *BBC News*, 17 March 2012, http://www.bbc.com/news/magazine-17390729.

6 Ben Bratton, 'iPhone City', in Leach, 'Digital Cities'.

7 Against the primacy of material form, we might therefore posit an alternative logic, and make a distinction between form – as in 'form for the sake of form' – and information. If, over the past few decades, we have seen a shift away from an obsession with pure form towards a set of more performative considerations, such as structural or environmental factors, whereby *form* is *informed* by *performative* constraints, should we not be recognising a further shift towards pure information?

8 It is now illegal to hold a cell phone while driving. Initially, however, most cell phones were known as 'car phones'. The name of one of the most prominent British outlets for cell phones, Carphone Warehouse, bears testimony to this early history.

9 For 'uber-ification', see http://schlaf.me/post/81679927670; http://
www.huffingtonpost.com/michael-boland/
apple-pays-real-killer-ap_b_6233828.html.

10 William Wilson, 'Uber Forced out of China', *Heritage Foundation*,
21 November 2016, https://www.heritage.org/asia/commentary/
uber-forced-out-china.

11 Mario Carpo, *The Second Digital Turn: Design Beyond Intelligence*,
Cambridge, MA: MIT Press, 2017.

12 'In different ways, today's digital avant-garde has already started
to use Big Data and computation to engage somehow the messy
discreteness of nature as it is, in its pristine, raw state – without
the mediation or the shortcut of elegant, streamlined mathematical
notations . . . The messy point-clouds and volumetric units of
design and calculation that result from these processes are today
increasingly shown in their apparently disjointed and fragmentary
state; and the style resulting from this mode of composition is often
called voxelization, or voxelation.' Carpo, *The Second Digital Turn*,
p. 66. This use of voxelisation, however, falls into the trap of
'architecturalisation': 'Likewise pixels and voxels – which do not
express the digital as such, but are effects of strategies to
"visualise" it – are seen by Carpo as literally becoming "digital"
architectural forms, as in the case of the Bolivar series of chairs
generated by Philippe Morel.' Neil Leach, 'There Is No Such Thing as
a Digital Building: A Critique of the Discrete', in Gilles Retsin (ed.),
'Discrete: Reappraising the Digital in Architecture', *AD* 258 (2019):
138.

13 For 'architecturalisation', see pp. 91–2.

14 Bratton, 'iPhone City'.

15 www.unfolded.ai. Despite the web address, however, the company
does not use AI at the moment.

16 Shan He, 'Data Driven Urbanism: The Balance Between Spatial
Intelligence and Design Craftsmanship', in Mark Burry (ed.), 'Urban
Futures: Designing the Digitalised City', *AD* 90, no. 3 (May–June
2020): 86–93.

17 He, 'Data Driven Urbanism'.

18 He, 'Data Driven Urbanism'.

19 Manuel Castells, *The Informational City: Information Technology,
Economic Restructuring and the Urban-Regional Process*, Oxford:
Blackwell, 1989.

20 Manuel Castells, *The Rise of the Network Society – The Information
Age: Economy, Society and Culture*, vol. 1, Malden, MA, and

Oxford: Blackwell, 1996; Manuel Castells, *The Power of Identity – The Information Age: Economy, Society and Culture*, vol. 2, Malden, MA, and Oxford: Blackwell, 1997; Manuel Castells, *End of Millennium –The Information Age: Economy, Society and Culture*, vol. 3, Malden, MA, and Oxford: Blackwell, 1998.

21 M. Batty, K. Axhausen, G. Fosca, A. Pozdnoukhov, A. Bazzani, M. Wachowicz, G. Ouzounis and Y. Portugali, 'Smart Cities of the Future', *European Physics Journal*, Special Topics 214 (2012): 481–518. Anthony Townsend stresses a similar point: 'Information technology needs to be part of the solution, but it does not solve any problems by itself, no matter how smart or powerful it is.' Townsend defines smart cities as 'places where information technology is combined with infrastructure, architecture, everyday objects, and even our bodies to address social, economic and environmental problems'. Anthony Townsend, *Smart Cities: Big Data, Civic Hackers, and the Quest for a New Utopia*, New York: Norton, 2014, p. 15.

22 Batty et al., 'Smart Cities of the Future', 481–518.

23 Benjamin Bratton, *The Stack: On Software and Sovereignty*, Cambridge, MA: MIT Press, 2017.

24 The devices that receive and transmit the information certainly operate in 3D Cartesian space. But could we not question whether the same applies to information itself, given that information is transmitted digitally, and the digital is immaterial and therefore non-dimensional?

25 Bratton, *The Stack*, p. 375.

26 Bratton, *The Stack*, pp. 70–1.

27 Jane Jacobs, *The Death and Life of the Great American Cities*, New York: Random House, 1961.

28 Benjamin Bratton, 'The City Wears Us. Notes on the Scope of Distributed Sensing and Sensation', *Glass-Bead Journal*, 2017, http://www.glass-bead.org/article/city-wears-us-notesscope-distributed-sensing-sensation/?lang=enview.

29 'Ambient intelligence is a vision of how ICTs will shape our future. It depicts a world of seamless intelligent environments, designed to understand and adapt to the presence of people and free them from manual control of their surroundings.' Kristrún Gunnarsdóttir and Michael Arribas-Ayllon, 'Ambient Intelligence: A Narrative in Search of Users', *Academia*, 2011, https://www.academia.edu/1080720/Ambient_Intelligence_an_innovation_narrative.

30 John Markoff, 'Mark Weiser, a Leading Computer Visionary, Dies at 46', *New York Times*, 1 May 1999.

31 For a vision of this future, see MIT Project Oxygen, 'Project Overview', http://oxygen.csail.mit.edu/Overview.html.

32 Examples in everyday life include the aquariums of fish often found in the waiting rooms of dental surgeries, for the specific purpose of calming patients down, and differential lighting used in the cabin of long-haul flight aircraft to wake passengers up, although these are simple one-way interactive processes.

33 There is, moreover, an established critique of surveillance that emanates from the thoughts of Jeremy Bentham and others. Shoshona Zuboff, *Surveillance Capitalism: The Fight for a Human Future at the New Frontier of Power*, New York: PublicAffairs, 2019.

34 Merritt Roe Smith and Leo Marx (eds), *Does Technology Drive History? The Dilemma of Technological Determinism*, Cambridge, MA: MIT Press, 1995.

35 See Neil Leach, 'London Mimetica/Camouflage London' (in Italian and English), *Domus* (January 2005): 90–5.

36 Steve Johnson, *Emergence: The Connected Lives of Ants, Cities and Software*. New York: Schribner, 2002.

37 See also John Holland, *Emergence: From Chaos to Order*, New York: Perseus, 1999; Mitchell Waldrop, *Complexity: The Emerging Science at the Edge of Order and Chaos*, New York and London: Simon and Schuster, 1992.

38 'An Emergent Interaction System consists of an environment in which a number of individual actors share some experience/phenomenon. Data originating from the actors and their behaviour is collected, transformed and fed back into the environment. The defining requirement of emergent interaction is that this feedback has some noticeable and interesting effect on the behaviour of the individuals and the collective – that something "emerges" in the interactions between the individuals, the collective, and the shared phenomenon as a result of introducing the feedback mechanism.' N. Andersson, A. Broberg, A. Bränberg, E. Jonsson, K. Holmlund and L.-E. Janlert, 'Emergent Interaction Systems – designing for emergence', paper presented at the Momuc workshop, 2003, Munich, Germany, http://www8.cs.umu.se/~bopspe/publications/ accessed 3/31/2014.

39 Within the field of architecture, multi-agent systems have become an important field of research. Neil Leach, and Roland Snooks (eds), *Swarm Intelligence: Architectures of Multi-Agent Systems*, Shanghai: Tongji University Press, 2017. The interest in a distributed model of design is forecast by Stan Allen when he cites Craig

Reynolds's work and suggests that swarm logic offers an insight into emergent methodologies: 'Crowds and swarms operate at the edge of control. Aside from the suggestive formal possibilities. I wish to suggest with these two examples that architecture could profitably shift its attention from its traditional top-down forms of control and begin to investigate the possibilities of a more fluid, bottom-up approach.' Stan Allen, 'From Object to Field', *Architectural Design* 67, no. 5/6 (May –June 1997): 24–31.

40 German neurophysiologist Wolf Singer has also made comparisons between the city and the brain. Wolf Singer, 'Die Architektur des Gehirns als Modell für komplexe Stadtstrukturen?', in C. Maar and F. Rötzer (eds), *Virtual Cities*, Basel: Birkhauser, 1997, pp. 153–61. This comparison inspired Coop Himmelb(l)au to develop a research group, Brain City Lab, which exhibited a model of a city at the Venice Biennale 2008. The model used computational methods to projection-map the behaviour of neurons on to a landscape model of the city. Coop Himmelb(l)au, 'Future Revisited', http://www.coop-himmelblau.at/architecture/projects/coop-himmelblau-future-revisited/.

41 See, for example, Michael Hensel, Achim Menges and Michael Weinstock, 'Emergence: Morphogenetic Design Strategies', *AD* (July–August 2004); Michael Weinstock, *The Architecture of Emergence: The Evolution of Form in Nature and Civilisation*, London: Wiley, 2010.

42 This is also sometimes referred to as populational behaviour. As Manuel DeLanda observes, 'The dynamics of populations of dislocations are very closely related to the population dynamics of very different entities, such as molecules in a rhythmic chemical reaction, termites in a nest-building colony, and perhaps even human agents in a market. In other words, despite the great difference in the nature and behavior of the components, a given population of interacting entities will tend to display similar collective behavior.' Manuel DeLanda, 'Deleuze and the Use of the Genetic Algorithm in Architecture', in Leach, *Designing for a Digital World*.

43 Leach and Snooks, *Swarm Intelligence*, p. 108.

44 Leach, Turnbull and Williams, *Digital Tectonics*, p. 72.

45 For examples, see Leach and Snooks, *Swarm Intelligence*; Neil Leach, 'Swarm Urbanism', in Neil Leach (ed.), *Digital Cities*, London: Wiley, 2009, pp. 56–63.

46 As argued elsewhere, these seemingly complex forms are in fact generated by relatively straightforward algorithms, whereas the spherical form of a simple soap bubble is far more complex, being generated, as it is, by the morphogenetic play of internal and external pressure, surface tension and so on. Leach, 'We Have Never Been Digital'.

47 Gilles Deleuze and Félix Guattari, 'City/State', in Leach, *Rethinking Architecture*, p. 297.

48 As I have argued elsewhere, 'This opens up an intriguing way of understanding the relationship between humans as "agents" within this system and the fabric of the city as a form of exoskeleton to human operations.' Neil Leach, 'Swarm Urbanism', in Leach, 'Digital Cities', *AD* 79, no. 4, Profile 200 (July–August 2009): 62.

49 Kevin Kelly, *Out of Control: The New Biology of Machines, Social Systems, and the Economic World*, New York: Basic Books, 1995.

50 John Holland, quoted by Johnson, *Emergence*, p. 27. Holland's point is that the water molecules making up the wave are constantly changing, but that the pattern of the wave remains the same, provided that the rock is still there and the water flows. John Holland, *Emergence: From Chaos to Order*, New York: Perseus, 1999, p. 29.

51 This model of the city maintaining a form of dynamic equilibrium echoes the larger model of the Earth as a self-regulating complex system, as postulated by James Lovelock. James Lovelock, *Gaia: A New Look at Life on Earth*, Oxford: Oxford University Press, 1979.

52 The term 'homeostasis' was coined by the American physiologist Walter Bradford Cannon in 1929 in reference to living systems. Significantly, Cannon chose the Ancient Greek term 'homeo' (meaning 'similar') over the alternative Ancient Greek term 'homo' (meaning 'the same'). By this, Cannon sought to distinguish human operations with their considerable variables from mechanical operations, such as in the case of the thermostat, which operate within a fixed system. Bradford Cannon, 'Organization for Physiological Homeostasis', *Physiological Reviews* 9, no. 3 (1929): 399–431.

53 Ashby predicted that the homeostat would even be able to play chess. William Ross Ashby, *Design for a Brain: The Origin of Adaptive Behavior*, London: Chapman and Hall, 1960.

54 There are echoes here of the work of Sigmund Freud, who had already referred to 'hydraulic construction of the unconscious' and its libidinal economy, such that 'the individual's conscious experience and behavior are the manifestation of a surging libidinal struggle between desire and repression'. John Daugman, 'Brain Metaphors and Brain Theory', in *Computational Neuroscience*, Cambridge, MA: MIT Press, 1993.

55 Alan Turing, letter to William Ashby, 1946, W. Ross Ashby Archive, http://www.rossashby.info/letters/turing.html.

56 Antonio Damasio, *The Strange Order of Things: Life, Feeling and the Making of Cultures*, New York: Vintage, 2019.

57 Antonio Damasio and Gil Carvalho, 'The Nature of Feelings: Evolutionary and Neurobiological Origins', *Neuroscience* 14 (2013): 143.

58 For sure, Damasio himself would never equate a city to the brain. Nor would he compare AI to the brain. In fact Damasio actually has a background in AI, and counts the renowned AI pioneer Warren McCulloch as his first American mentor. Indeed at the time, Damasio shared some of the early excitement in neurobiology, computation and AI. And yet now he is aware of the shortcomings of this view, in that it overlooks the importance of the body. 'In retrospect, however, it had little to offer by way of a realistic view of what human minds look and feel like. How could it, given that the respective theory disengaged the dried up mathematical description of the activity of neurons from the thermodynamics of life processes? Boolean algebra has its limits when it comes to making minds.' Damasio, *The Strange Order of Things*, p. 240.

59 Previously I have also explored the possibility of the house operating as a form of brain: Neil Leach, 'Emergent Interactivities: From the primitive hut to the cerebral hut', *Proceedings of the 34th Annual Conference of the Association for Computer Aided Design in Architecture*, 23–25 October 2014, n.p.p.: n.p., pp. 145–52.

60 Kelleher, *Deep Learning*, p. 79.

61 Alibaba is a Chinese multinational conglomerate holding company based in Hangzhou. It specialises in ecommerce, and could be considered as the Chinese rival to Amazon, although, unlike Amazon, Alibaba is not involved in direct sales and does not own any warehouses. https://www.alibaba.com/.

62 Liu Feng, 'City Brain, a New Architecture of Smart City Based on the Internet Brain', https://arxiv.org/ftp/arxiv/papers/1710/1710.04123.pdf.

63 https://www.tomtom.com/en_gb/traffic-index/hangzhou-traffic.

64 Abigail Beall, 'In China, Alibaba's data-hungry AI is controlling (and watching) cities', *Wired*, 30 May 2018, https://www.wired.co.uk/article/alibaba-city-brain-artificial-intelligence-china-kuala-lumpur=.

65 https://www.alibabacloud.com/solutions/intelligence-brain/city.

66 Blog Post, 'City Brain Now in 23 Cities in Asia', *Alibaba Cloud Blog*, 28 October 2019, https://www.alibabacloud.com/blog/city-brain-now-in-23-cities-in-asia_595479.

as wristwatches, rings, earrings and other body ornaments', https://kurzweilai.net/images/How-My-Predictions-Are-Faring.pdf.

33 https://kurzweilai.net/images/How-My-Predictions-Are-Faring.pdf.

34 'Cables are disappearing. Communication between components, such as pointing devices, microphones, displays, printers, and the occasional keyboard uses short-distance wireless technology . . . Computers routinely include wireless technology to plug into the ever-present worldwide network, providing reliable, instantly available, very high bandwidth communication', https://kurzweilai.net/images/How-My-Predictions-Are-Faring.pdf.

35 'Computers routinely include moving picture image cameras and are able to reliably identify their owners from their faces', https://kurzweilai.net/images/How-My-Predictions-Are-Faring.pdf.

36 'Computer displays built into eyeglasses are also used. These specialized glasses allow users to see the normal visual environment, while creating a virtual image that appears to hover in front of the viewer', https://kurzweilai.net/images/How-My-Predictions-Are-Faring.pdf.

37 Drake Baer, '5 amazing predictions by futurist Ray Kurzweil that came true – and 4 that haven't', *Business Insider*, 20 October 2015.

38 Yuli Ban, 'Kurzweil's 2009 is our 2019', *Reddit*, 2019, https://www.reddit.com/r/singularity/comments/94dkea/kurzweils_2009_is_our_2019/.

39 https://kurzweilai.net/images/How-My-Predictions-Are-Faring.pdf.

40 Kurzweil, *The Age of Spiritual Machines*, p. 406. In *The Hitchhiker's Guide to the Galaxy* series of books and movies, Douglas Adams includes Babel Fish that are inserted into the ear to provide instantaneous translation. https://hitchhikers.fandom.com/wiki/Babel_Fish.

41 Kurzweil, *The Age of Spiritual* Machines, pp. 410–11.

42 Kurzweil, *The Singularity is Near*, https://singularityhub.com/2017/03/31/can-futurists-predict-the-year-of-the-singularity/#sm.00001ep69rsevnd56vi0hrvmkpsor.

43 Christianna Reedy, 'Kurzweil Predicts That the Singularity Will Happen in 2045', *Futurism*, 5 October 2017, futurism.com/kurzweil-claims-that-the-singularity-will-happen-by-2045.

44 Shanahan, *The Technological Singularity*.

45 Stanislaw Ulam, 'Tribute to John von Neumann', *Bulletin of the American Mathematical Society* 64, no. 3, Pt. 2 (May 1958).

46 Vincent Vernon, *The Technological Singularity*, n.p.p.: n.p., 1993.

47 http://www.kurzweilai.net/the-law-of-accelerating-returns.

48 David Chalmers, 'The Singularity: A Philosophical Analysis', *Journal of Consciousness Studies* 17 (2010): 7–65.

49 Christianna Reedy, 'Kurzweil Predicts That the Singularity Will Happen in 2045', *Futurism*, 5 October 2017. futurism.com/kurzweil-claims-that-the-singularity-will-happen-by-2045.

50 Reedy, 'Kurzweil Predicts That the Singularity Will Happen in 2045'.

51 'The Turing Test, 1950', *The Alan Turing Internet Scrapbook*, https://www.turing.org.uk/scrapbook/test.html.

52 Despite the confusing message conveyed in the title of Walsh's book, we are certainly not there yet. Walsh, *Machines that Think*.

53 From this perspective, it is somewhat surprising that an expert on AI, such as Toby Walsh, should entitle a book about the past, present and future of AI, *Machines that Think: The Future of Artificial Intelligence*. A more plausible title would have been *Machines that Might Eventually Think*. Most would argue that for the moment, at least, computers cannot think. Walsh, *Machines that Think*.

54 David Chalmers, 'How Do You Explain Consciousness?', TED Talk, 2014, https://www.ted.com/talks/david_chalmers_how_do_you_explain_consciousness/transcript.

55 Justin Weinberg, 'Philosophers on GPT-3 (with replies by GPT-3)', *Daily Nous*, 30 July 2020, https://dailynous.com/2020/07/30/philosophers-gpt-3/.

56 Nick Bostrom goes on to identify three manifestations of superintelligence: 'Speed superintelligence: A system that can do all that a human intellect can do, but faster . . . Collective superintelligence: A system composed of a large number of smaller intellects such that the system's overall performance across many very general domains vastly outstrips that of any current cognitive system . . . Quality superintelligence: A system that is at least as fast as a human mind and vastly qualitatively smarter.' Bostram admits, however, that there are other ways of understanding superintelligence. Nick Bostrom, *Superintelligence: Paths, Dangers, Strategies*, Oxford: Oxford University Press, 2016, pp. 64, 65, 68.

57 Bostrom, *Superintelligence*, p. 26.

58 'Elon's Message on Artificial Superintelligence – ASI', *Science Time*, 24 October 2020, https://www.youtube.com/watch?v=ZCeOsdcQObl&feature=youtu.be. See also Amber Case, 'We Are All Cyborgs Now', *TEDWomen*, 2010, https://www.ted.com/talks/amber_case_we_are_all_cyborgs_now?language=en.

59 Irving John Good, 'Speculations Concerning the First Ultraintelligent Machine', in Franz Alt and Morris Rubinoff (eds), *Advances in Computers*, New York: Academic Press, 1965, p. 33.

60 Elon Musk quoted in Ricki Harris, 'Elon Musk: Humanity is a Kind of Biological Boot Loader for AI', *Wired*, 1 September 2019, https://www.wired.com/story/elon-musk-humanity-biological-boot-loader-ai/.

61 Arthur Ellis, *Teaching and Learning Elementary Social Studies*, Boston: Allyn & Bacon, 1970, p. 431.

62 Andy Clark reminds us about this in relation to predictive perception. Clark, *Surfing Uncertainty*.

63 Turing, 'Computing Machinery and Intelligence', 433–60.

64 This is also confusing, as 2029 is the date that Kurzweil gives for AI achieving 'human level intelligence' and not AGI. Ford, *Architects of Intelligence*, p. 528.

65 For an overview of different time estimates, see https://aiimpacts.org/ai-timeline-surveys/.

66 Kanta Dihal, Andrew Hessel, Amy Robinson Sterling and Francesca Rossi, 'Visionary Interviews', in Woods, Livingston and Uchida , *AI: More Than Human*.

67 Ford, *Architects of Intelligence*, p. 436.

68 Dihal, Hessel, Sterling and Rossi, 'Visionary Interviews', in Woods, Livingston and Uchida, *AI: More than Human*, p. 210.

69 It should be noted that 'human level intelligence' does not require consciousness, whereas AGI does. Ford, *Architects of Intelligence*, p. 528.

70 Russell in Ford, *Architects of Intelligence*, p. 48.

71 Kelly argues that intelligence is not one-dimensional, but is constituted by 'many types and modes of cognition, each one a continuum'. Intelligence, for Kelly, is effectively an eco-system, involving many different types of thinking, and suffused throughout the whole body. Kevin Kelly, 'The Myth of a Superhuman AI', *Wired*, 25 April, 2017, https://www.wired.com/2017/04/the-myth-of-a-superhuman-ai/

72 Hassabis in Ford, *Architects of Intelligence*, p. 176.

73 Roger Penrose, 'Consciousness is Not a Computation', interview with Lex Fridmann, 4 April 2020, https://www.youtube.com/watch?v=hXgqik6HXc0.

74 Anil Seth, 'Your Brain Hallucinates Your Conscious Reality', TED Talk, April 2017, https://www.ted.com/talks/anil_seth_your_brain_hallucinates_your_conscious_reality?language=en.

75 Ray Kurzweil, *How to Create a Mind: The Secrets of Human Thought Revealed*, New York: Penguin, 2012.

76 Eric Elliott, 'What's it like to be a computer: an interview with GPT-3', 18 September 2020, https://www.youtube.com/watch?v= PqbB07n_uQ4&ab_channel=EricElliott.

77 I am grateful to Casey Rehm for this observation.

78 Max Tegmark, *Life 3.0: Being Human in the Age of Artificial Intelligence*, New York: Vintage, 2017, p. 314.

79 'Elon Musk's Message on Artificial Superintelligence – ASI', *Science Time*, 24 October 2020, https://www.youtube.com/watch?v=ZCeOs dcQObl&feature=youtu.be.

80 What we could probably predict with a degree of certainty, however, is that a 'post-AI' movement will emerge, just as a 'post-digital' movement has emerged. It is far from clear, however, whether we are even 'digital' yet, still less 'post-digital'. If there is anything that AI has taught us, it is that the domain of the digital is constantly evolving. As such, claims that we are completely familiar with the digital, or maybe even *beyond* the digital, seem a little premature. Rumours of the death of the digital are greatly exaggerated. Leach, 'We Have Never Been Digital'.

81 Brooks in Ford, *Architects of Intelligence*, p. 423.

82 Brooks in Ford, *Architects of Intelligence*, p. 441.

83 Bill Gates quoted in 'Introduction' in Leach, *Designing for a Digital World*, p. 6.

84 However, not all predictions about the digital revolution have proved correct. Many had hoped that it would lead automatically to a culture of progressive experimentation and a better world. In fact it just gave us spam. Others had predicted that it would lead to a densification of our cities. And yet, as Andrew Gillespie has noted, it just led to out-of-town facilities, such as shopping centres and Amazon warehouses, while the shops in the inner city are being threatened more and more by the development of online shopping. Andrew Gillespie, 'Digital Lifestyles and the Future City', in Leach, *Designing for a Digital World*, pp. 68–72.

85 'My own prediction is that by 2020 we won't even use the word "computation" because it will be everywhere.' 'Interview' in Neil Leach and Xu Weiguo (eds), *Design Intelligence: Advanced Computational Techniques for Architecture*, Beijing: CABP, 2010, p. 8.

86 This argument comes from Jean Baudrillard, who contends that once everything becomes aesthetic, the word 'art' becomes meaningless: 'When everything becomes aesthetic, nothing is either beautiful or ugly any longer, and art itself disappears.' Jean Baudrillard, 'Transpolitics, Transsexuality, Transaesthetics', trans.

Michael Valentin, in William Stearns and William Chaloupka (eds), *The Disappearance of Art and Politics*, London: Macmillan, 1992, p. 10. But the argument could also be applied to other fields: 'When everything becomes historical, nothing is historical any more. When everything becomes political, nothing is political any more. And likewise when everything becomes aesthetic, nothing is aesthetic any more. We live in a transhistorical, transpolitical and transaesthetic world. As each category grows swollen and distended, a condition of obesity exists, and the contents are obliterated. Everything has been xeroxised into infinity. In this ecstasy of replication, this society of saturation, events have been lost in the void of information, deprived of all meaning.' Neil Leach, *Millennium Culture*, London: Ellipsis, 1999, p. 24.

87 McCarthy adds, 'I had a vague feeling that I'd heard the phrase before, but in all these years I have never been able to track it down.' N. J. Nielson, transcript of 'Oral History of John McCarthy', interview by Nils Nilsson on 12 September 2007 at and for the Computer History Museum, Mountain View, California, http://www.nasonline.org/publications/biographical-memoirs/memoir-pdfs/mccarthy-john.pdf; reprinted in N. J. Nielson, *John McCarthy: A Biographical Memoir*, Washington, DC: National Academy of Sciences, 2012.

88 Walsh, *Machines that Think*, p. 17.

89 Stibel, *Wired for Thought*.

90 Turing, letter to William Ashby.

91 Geoffrey Hinton interviewed by Martin Ford, in Ford, *Architects of Intelligence*, p. 80.

92 Hassabis and Hui, 'AlphaGo', p. 88.

93 Philip Yuan, Mike Xie, Neil Leach, Jiawei Yao, Xiang Wang (eds), *Architectural Intelligence*, Singapore: Springer, 2020.

94 'Collectively they could be referred to as *architectural intelligence* (AI). The word AI Tect encompasses two meanings: *architectural intelligence* and *artificial intelligence*.' Watanabe, 'AI Tect: Can AI Make Designs?', pp. 68–75.

95 https://eyesofthecity.net/ai-chitect/.

96 Steenson uses the term to refer to the contributions of four architects: Christopher Alexander, Richard Saul Wurman, Cedric Price and Nicholas Negroponte. Molly Wright Steenson, *Architectural Intelligence: How Designers and Architects Created the Digital Landscape*, Cambridge, MA: MIT Press, 2017.

97 Yuan, Xie, Leach, Yao and Wang, *Architectural Intelligence*, p. 3.

98   Mark Burry, *Expiatory Church of the Sagrada Familia: Antonio Gaudí*, London: Phaidon, 1992; Winfried Nerdinger, *Frei Otto: Complete Works*, Basel: Birkhaüser, 2005.

99   This was the case in certain studios in the Department of Architecture at the University of Cambridge.

100 As Maria Dantz comments, 'I remember when I started studying in my first two semesters our professors were very adamant that we had to draw by hand. I don't think that anyone in Bauhaus University still does that. In the same way that it is now normal to use ArchiCad, Revit and stuff like that, hopefully AI tools will be in that same vein.' Zoom conversation, 6 May 2020.

101 Leach, 'We Have Never Been Digital'.

102 Christensen, 'Global PropTech Interview #5'. Despite numerous attempts to obtain further details from Spacemaker about their working methods, no information was forthcoming.

103 See Neil Leach, *The Death of the Architect*, London: Bloomsbury, 2021.

104 MIT Project Oxygen, 'Project Overview', http://oxygen.csail.mit.edu/Overview.html.

105 See p. 117.

106 Haley, 'The Future of Design Powered by AI'.

107 He, 'Urban Experiment', p. 99

108 Dantz, Zoom conversation, 6 May 2020

109 Havard Haukeland, Spacemaker AI, Zoom conversation, 6 May 2020.

110 See p. 121.

111 See p. 116.

Index

Page numbers: Figures are given in *italics* and notes as [page number] n. [note number].